T

Cover by Stephanie Welch
Photographs of road signs by Tom Rae. Yes, he's my dad. No, I
didn't pay him.

First published in electronic form (http://english2american.com)
1997
First published in book form in 2008

ISBN 978-0-9815790-0-9

ABOUT THE AUTHOR

Chris Rae is a Scot currently living and working in Seattle, WA, U.S.A. This is a picture of him looking rugged and outdoorsy. He is married, so whoever you are please stop sending that stuff. It's not pleasant to unwrap over breakfast and it must be playing havoc with your digestive health.

To Nimrod Fartelchease, figurehead of the anonymous masses
who have lent me their time and energy.

CONTENTS

INTRODUCTION

Like many other successful intercontinental jet-setters, I once started to compile a list of British words which seemed to be unfamiliar to Americans. My personal website was disappointingly lacking in content, so to bolster it I posted my big list of words up there. Strangers began sending me emails whining about the inaccuracies and blatant lies I'd incorporated, as though I were being paid to keep it up to date or something. Bastards.

Whilst pacing the living room trying to think of some way of making money, I couldn't help thinking about that fine website of mine. Surely that must be worth something? Well, here it is. Fingers crossed.

Throughout this book I've used British English terms and spelling. The upside of this is, I hope, that you get some sort of context for a lot of the words defined in the dictionary. The downside is that looking up a word may result in you looking up another two. You'll have to live with that. Your time is cheap to me.

There are many hundreds of British words which are not in the dictionary part. I've tried to restrict myself to words which are known and understood throughout the whole of the U.K. When talking about British language idiosyncrasies some people delight in trotting out phrases that no Brit would ever have heard unless they lived in a particular part of Dorset, in a particular street, and were present during a particular incident in the fourteenth century. The words and phrases in the dictionary portion of this book should all be ones which would be recognised and understood by any Brit.

This is a work of reference, but I make no claims concerning its accuracy. Many of the "facts" contained herein are simply quoted verbatim from random people on the internet, with little or no effort made to verify their validity. I've been writing this steadily over the last ten years – sometimes I was tired, sometimes I was emotional and quite often I was drunk. This is not the OED.

POLITICAL GEOGRAPHY OF THE U.K.

One thing Brits really enjoy is whining about Americans calling the whole of the United Kingdom "England." It's usually an opener into some diatribe about Americans being xenophobic and ethnocentric.

Truth be told, a lot of Brits have a rather dismal understanding of their country and its constituent parts – try asking one whether Scotland is in the United Nations, or whether Northern Ireland is in Britain.

So, here we go. The United Kingdom is a country. It gets to do all sorts of neat things, like be in the United Nations, and the European Union and stuff. The Brits are the lucky owners of the longest official country name in the world: "The United Kingdom of Great Britain and Northern Ireland." So far so good. If anyone else looks like they're going to

beat them, I think they could always stick a "Democratic Republic of" in there. Now for the complicated bits.

The United Kingdom consists of Britain and Northern Ireland, and is governed from London. "Britain," or more properly "Great Britain," means the mainland countries: England, Scotland and Wales. Are these proper countries? Well, that's a lot trickier to answer than you might think. In most political affairs, they behave as one country (the U.K.) but in some other things, notably sport, you'll find separate English, Scottish and Welsh teams. Within Britain, Scotland and Wales do have their own regional mini-parliaments with some legislative power, but generally they're told what to do by the main U.K. government, based in London. If you wanted to, you could see them as state legislature and the U.K. as federal, though in reality they don't have as much autonomy as the American states do.

Given that Scotland and Wales have their own pretend governments, you'd think that England would be pissed off about not having one too. The truth is that, given that England encompasses more than 80 percent of the U.K. population, the U.K. parliament usually adequately reflects what England wants.

To cover some popular misconceptions: Scotland and Wales are quite definitely not in England. English, Scottish and Welsh people are all British, but only people who come from England are English. These disparities can be equated reasonably closely to the interweaving of the United States - calling a Welshman "English" is pretty similar to calling a Texan an Alaskan. At least, it would be if Texans hated Alaskans.

And then there's Northern Ireland. This is the northeast section of the island of Ireland, around Belfast. The rest of Ireland is a separate country, officially called "Eire" (its Irish name) but quite often just called "Ireland" (its English name). Northern Ireland is governed by the United Kingdom. How did the U.K. end up governing a small chunk of its next-door neighbour? Well, the whole of Ireland was given to England by Pope Adrian in the twelfth century, as a gift. He'd been given it the Christmas before by a distant relative and it had just been languishing in a cupboard. The Irish were pretty furious about this, and fought periodically against British rule until the First World War, when a bloody attempt at revolt provoked Britain to create two parliaments - one for Northern Ireland, and another one for the rest. The country of southern Ireland, Eire, became independent in 1937 but Northern Ireland remained a British protectorate. Quite a few people in Northern Ireland were rather angry about this, and have been letting off bombs now and again to remind the Brits of their unhappiness. The pro/anti-British divide in Northern Ireland is very much down religious lines — the Protestants want to stay with the Brits, and the Catholics don't. Historically the population has been predominantly Protestant, but the Catholics are breeding like only Catholics can and eventually the balance will inevitably swing. Like Scotland and Wales, Northern Ireland has its own mini-parliament.

The upshot of all this is that the terms "United Kingdom" and "Britain" are pretty much interchangeable. The people who live in the U.K. are always called the British, rather than United Kingdomish. Or United Kingdomites. This, coupled with the fact that "The United Kingdom" is a crap name for a country, means that the whole country is more often called "Britain." I don't think anyone cares that they're subconsciously leaving out Northern Ireland. It's just some angry bearded men, a couple of bombs and the remains of the De Lorean factory.

THE WAY GOVERNMENT WORKS

Aside from the toy governments in Scotland, Northern Ireland and Wales (see "Political Geography of the U.K."), the U.K. is governed in a similar way to most other modern constitutional monarchies. I'll try to draw analogies with the American system, because it's the American market that I'm broadly aiming this book at. They've got all the money, apparently.

History

Ages ago, Britain was split into lots of little Kingdoms. These fought with each other like normal human beings, and eventually resolved into the comparatively stable kingdoms of Scotland and England, around the year 1000. Heaven knows where Wales fitted in. I doubt anyone had noticed it yet.

Apart from having banquets and orgies, the main duty of a monarch is to produce heirs to the throne. Unfortunately Elizabeth I of England entirely forgot to do this and so, when she died in 1603, the throne of England was handed to James I of Scotland, whose great grandmother's best friend had once done yoga with Elizabeth's mother. England wasn't put under the control of Scotland – they retained their own system of government and all it meant for James was being able to call himself "King of Great Britain," lots of red-eye flights into Heathrow and interminable baggage checks.

Despite a brief foray into military dictatorship, the whole country was so pleased to have just the one king stealing their money that Scotland and England were united into a single United Kingdom in 1707, which exists to the present day.

The Royal Family

Nowadays, the Royal Family aren't really involved in running the country. The monarch (currently Queen Elizabeth II) has a weekly audience with the Prime Minister, during which they talk about recent sporting events, or nip down to the pub for a swift half and some dominos. Whilst nominally the reigning monarch is allowed to dissolve parliament, make treaties and such like, it's a bit doubtful as to whether they'd really be able to put any of those things into practice.

The Royal Family has three main functions in modern Britain. The first is to invoke antagonism amongst the chattering classes about what the bloody Royal Family ever does for anyone. Bloody social leeches. The second is to provide the tourist industry with ceremonial events, tea towels, commemorative spoons, postcards and other overpriced memorabilia which will be snapped up by enthusiastic tourists and displayed in homes all over the modern world. Their third is to generate C-grade scandal for the chattering classes by having sex with supermodels, smoking pot or making obliquely racist comments on television. Elizabeth II's son, Charles, was hampered by his looks from humping any supermodels and prevented by his personality from scoring weed, although his children, Princes William and Harry, are considerably better looking and attempting to make amends. Elizabeth's husband, Prince Philip, is a much more enthusiastic scandalmonger and is famous for asking an Australian aborigine whether they still threw spears at each other, and telling British students in China that "if you stay here much longer, you'll get all slitty-eyed."

Parliament

The real governing of the U.K. happens in parliament. Parliament is split into two sections: the House of Commons and the House of Lords. Both of these are open proceedings, with the participants surrounded by public galleries usually full of budding terrorists trying to map the ventilation systems.

The House of Commons

The House of Commons is a bunch of six hundred or so elected Members of Parliament (M.P.s) from a mixture of political parties, each representing a particular area of the U.K. At General Elections, British citizens only get one vote, and that's for their local M.P. Their M.P. will most likely belong to a political party, and so Brits run the risk of electing a blithering moron to represent their region just because they belonged to the party they wanted to be in power. Of course, Americans are quite capable of electing a blithering moron to be president when that was the only election going on at the time, so perhaps now's not the time to pass judgement on the British system.

The House of Commons is essentially a mixture between the Senate and the House of Representatives. They sit on most weekdays in London's Palace of Westminster and shout at each other about the topics of the day. There's a lot more shouting in the British political process than there is in the American one — they even have a special employee, the Speaker, whose primary task is to shout "order, order!" when the yelling gets a bit too much.

The political party with the most M.P.s is the one that gets to be in government. The leader of that party gets to be Prime Minister. As well as representing their various regions, M.P.s from the ruling party are also allocated other positions in the government (Minister for Transport, Minister for Education, etc.). Not to be outdone, the opposition party gets to do this too — to distinguish their pretend ones from the real ones, their titles are preceded by the term "Shadow" — Shadow Minister for the Environment, Shadow Health Minister, et cetera.

The Chamber of Commons is a long room — the intention is that the governing party sit on one side and the opposition sit on the other. Anyone from other parties has to just squeeze in where they can. The more important people are closer to the front, and so anyone with a ministerial position is known as a "front-bencher" and someone who's just sitting around representing their local constituents is a "back-bencher." Not all M.P.s are in Parliament every day, but parties will sometimes recall M.P.s from their constituencies if they need help with a particular upcoming vote.

The Voting Process

The purpose of the House of Commons is to discuss and pass Bills. Determining exactly what Bills may encompass involves lots of interminably dull details, but they generally cover the laws of the land, taxation and spending. Once a Bill is proposed, the House of Commons debate it for a while before having a vote. All M.P.s present in the Chamber are cued to shout a verbal "aye" or "no." If it wasn't entirely obvious who won that, the M.P.s then file into "aye" or "no" areas in the side of the Chamber and are counted. Sometimes MPs are directed how to vote by their party; sometimes they aren't.

The House of Lords

The House of Lords is a motley bunch of drunken octogenarian ex-politicians, hereditary title holders, religious leaders, serial cat rapists and deranged millionaires appointed at the whim of the political parties without any sort of democratic process at all. Think of it as Britain's Supreme Court. Unlike the Chamber of Commons, the Lords' Chamber is ornately decorated with red leather, splendid chandeliers and a gilded relief ceiling.

The purpose of the House of Lords is to serve as a sanity check on Bills passed by the House of Commons, a task unsuited to most of its members. Although an inebriated second opinion can often be a useful wake-up call, various Acts of Parliament have served to restrict the power of the House of Lords to merely the ability to delay Commons Bills (they can no longer reject them) — and several categories of Bill are deemed important enough for them not to be allowed to even do that.

The Constitution

Britain doesn't have a constitution. Why it's called a Constitutional Monarchy I've no idea. Parliament is entirely within its rights to decide that all dogs should be painted green, anyone found washing their car on a Saturday should be hung from the neck until dead and all citizens should be allowed to buy handguns from supermarkets. The nearest thing the Brits have to an emergency-release valve on the entire Parliament is the monarch, who might at that point decide to step in and exercise some of their long-forgotten rights to dissolve Parliament and repaint dogs.

IS BRITAIN IN THE EUROPEAN UNION?

Most countries in Europe are members of an organisation called the European Union (E.U.), which aims to help the region take advantage of economies of scale and cooperate for mutual benefit. It has its own currency, the euro, which many but not all of its members have adopted. Both the United Kingdom and Eire are members of the E.U.

Eire thinks the European Union is great, and they've converted all of their street signs to kilometres and adopted the euro currency. They've recently started an extensive government-funded programme to give every member of the Irish population a euro symbol tattoo on a posterial cheek of their choice.

Britain thinks that the European Union legislature is made up of a bunch of snotty French tossers who want to mess around making laws about the curvature of bananas and steal their money. There's a part of the British psyche which hasn't quite realised that Britain is no longer a world superpower, and so Brits are not so keen about being pushed around by the rest of Europe. Especially the French.

The downside of falling out with Europe is that lately the U.K. has had to make friends with America, which means spending your free weekends invading people. Eventually the U.K. will probably have to start toeing the line a bit more dutifully as far as the European Union goes, but for the moment they're members mainly in order to defeat the beast from within.

WEIGHTS AND MEASURES

Is Britain Metric?

Yes.

No.

Britain's relationship with the metric system is much like an old lady's relationship with a door-to-door vacuum cleaner salesman. Wait, I haven't finished. After peering suspiciously at him through the spy-hole for some minutes, she listens to the first part of his sales pitch through the letter box. Tired after a day of dusting, she resignedly unhooks one of many chains on the door and warily hears out the second segment of his routine through the inch of doorway she's made available. As she begins to unbolt the second chain, she knows in her heart of hearts that within ten minutes he's going to be making himself a cup of tea and strolling around her living room demonstrating the wonders of the Electrolux 5000. It's probably a fine device but oh, why all this change. Why all this upheaval? What was *wrong*?

The salesman has been strolling around the living room for several hundred years now, and Britain is pretty much metric apart from large distances, which are still measured in miles. There is also a large worn patch on the carpet. The food Brits buy in supermarkets is labelled in kilograms, although often they will show supplementary text showing the weight in pounds. Road signs, speed limits and such are measured in miles, but shorter distances are often measured in metres. Temperature is universally measured in Celsius, although people over fifty will quite often be more familiar with Fahrenheit.

It's more a question of when Britain will change to kilometres than whether they will, but it's quite possible that isn't going to be very soon. Swapping everything over is a considerable expense and given the British public's normal conservative reaction to change, it's going to be tough for any government to make a case for spending millions of pounds on messing around with road signs instead of finding a cure for cancer, doing something bad to the French or helping friendless despots invade other countries.

Weight for food and other household-type things is measured fairly ubiquitously in kilograms (kilos). Larger weights (cars and such) are measured in "tons." I put this in quotes because I think most Brits who use the term are unaware of whether they mean metric tonnes (1000kg) or imperial tons (2240lbs, or 1016kg). Weight of human beings, and only human beings, is measured in stones (14 lbs).

The curious end result of this semi-metric state is that British children learn all of the short distances in metric units and all of the long distances in miles. So whilst little Jimmy would know that his average stride took him 0.7 metres and that his house was a mile away, he'd sadly not have the faintest idea how to tell you how many steps it would take him to get home.

Writing the Date

Like the rest of the world apart from America, the British write the date in the format day/month/year. Writing the date in the American month/day/year style will be greeted with as much hilarity as writing the time in the format minute: hour: second.

BRITISH CURRENCY

One of the things that unites The United Kingdom is its common currency. Well, that and a dislike for the French. The four nations of the United Kingdom all use the Pound Sterling (£), which in turn is divided into one hundred "pennies," or "pence." The "Sterling" part of the name derives from the fact that it was once represented by a pound in weight of sterling silver (silver, with some copper added to strengthen it); now it's unanimously known simply as the "pound." The coins come in the denominations of one and two pence (copper-coloured), five, ten, twenty and fifty pence (silver), one pound (gold) and two pounds, which is a silver coin inset into a larger gold disc. All of these have the Queen's head on one side, and some sort of other design on the other. Not her real head, just a picture of it. The design on the other side could be one of quite a few things — different ones are often used to symbolise seminal events or as a nod towards each of the various "nations" in the U.K. These nods are usually in the form of a lion for England, a leek for Wales, a thistle for Scotland and "flax" for Northern Ireland. Whatever the fuck that is. The notes come in denominations of five, ten, twenty and fifty pounds. In everyday speech, you're as likely to hear the word "quid" as you are "pound" – this is the British equivalent of the American "buck".

While Scotland and Northern Ireland aren't allowed to have their own currency, some of their regional banks are allowed to print their own banknotes. These notes are technically not legal tender in England, but will normally be accepted without a problem. It's worth trying to generally stick to English notes if you're travelling around a lot.

The occasional store in the U.K. will take euros but it's normally to make a political point more than anything, and on the whole you're unlikely to get very far with them within Britain.

REGIONAL LANGUAGES AND ACCENTS

Gaelic, the traditional language of Scotland, is closely related to Irish and was spoken throughout Scotland from around the sixth century until the fifteenth, when English began to take over. Gaelic is a soft, cooing, mellifluous language that sounds as if it were invented mainly for soothing animals.

The 2001 census showed that just over 1% of Scots spoke Gaelic. They were all, without exception, irritating bearded people who want to drone on about heritage and force the government to spend millions of pounds making dual-language road signs that nobody ever reads. The census showed that they lived with their mothers, and at home they secretly spoke English.

Welsh, on the other hand, is actually spoken in Wales. The 2001 census indicated that 21% of Welsh people speak the Welsh language – an increase from the previous count, implying that the language is on the ascent. This doesn't mean that 21% of them use Welsh as a first language, and in reality the vast majority of everyday life in Wales is conducted in English. However, if you were to visit Wales there's a reasonable chance that you'd hear a conversation going on in Welsh, even if it was just about your ridiculous hair, or how fat your child was. Welsh is another soft, vowelly language, although it is punctuated regularly by guttural phlegm-gargling noises, causing speakers to be often mistaken for drunks speaking Hebrew.

The Welsh toy parliament issues all of its literature in two languages, and the teaching of Welsh is compulsory in schools in Wales up to the age of sixteen. There's a Welsh-language BBC radio station and a Welsh-language TV channel.

Neither Wales nor Scotland is nearly as bilingual as Canada, or even Southern California.

There are vast regional differences in accents across the U.K., and even across comparatively small physical distances. A Scot can easily tell the difference between an Edinburgh accent and a Glasgow one, though the cities are barely fifty miles apart. Likewise, someone from Sheffield need only hear two words from a Barnsley resident to know that he's going to need a good shoeing outside the pub after closing time. As you move further away, the accuracy diminishes — a Scot could tell a Northern English accent from a Southern one, but would be unlikely to tell the difference between a Salford accent and a Bolton one. This doesn't mean that Brits are somehow born with a natural ear for accents, as they are unable to tell the difference between a Texan accent, a New York accent and a Canadian one.

COCKNEY RHYMING SLANG

Cockney rhyming slang is a pretty simple if somewhat odd affair. It basically consists of a couplet of words, the second of which rhymes with the word you're actually aiming at. For example, the word "glasses" is represented by the phrase "Aristotle Onassis," and the word "look" by the phrase "butcher's hook." To further complicate matters, you can optionally use only the first word of the couplet to refer to the word you're ultimately aiming at - so your Aristotles are your glasses, and you can take a butchers out of them at the scenery once you've put them on.

Cockney rhyming slang is talked about more often than it is actually used. Some phrases are in fairly common usage country-wide — you're quite likely to hear people saying "butchers" to mean "look," or "porkies" to mean "lies" (pork pies), but you're unlikely to hear anyone talking about putting on their Aristotles. I've tried to put the most widely used ones into the dictionary. Whether I've succeeded or not I'm not too bothered; you've paid for it now so I couldn't care two hoots whether it turns out to be useful. Perhaps there'll be more in next year's edition when you buy that.

EATING OUT

British restaurants love American customers. This is because the customary tip in the U.S. is around twice what it is in the U.K. This in turn is because Americans are used to paying for a truly exemplary level of service from restaurant employees who have seen the actual menu before, can remember a list of more than two things and do not hate everyone. Americans dining in the U.K. must console themselves with this financial saving while they stand at the bar waiting to order food, try to find someone who will explain where the loo is or wander aimlessly around the back of the restaurant wondering from where it was they were supposed to collect their own goddamned cutlery.

British Food

British food is world famous. It's well known throughout the modern world for being bland, uninspiring and poorly prepared. Traditional British dishes consist of a lump of meat, a dollop of potatoes, perhaps some gravy and a carrot. British food is the subsistence food of the fourteenth century, and therefore not so appealing to people who want a romantic expensive meal on Valentine's day that they are not intending keeping in salt over the winter and sharing with the cows.

This isn't to say that there isn't good food in the U.K. Of course there is, just like there is anywhere. There is a lot of excellent French and Italian food in the U.K. There's also a great deal of what the Brits lovingly call "Indian" or "Chinese" food. These are essentially British versions of the food that people eat in India and China, and bear several mixed levels of resemblance to the cuisine of those countries. One very popular British Indian curry, the "Balti," was actually invented in the U.K. and never existed in India. No doubt somebody will open a "British restaurant" in Bangalore selling them.

GOING OUT DRINKING

Drinking is an enormous part of U.K. culture. Brits require a couple of drinks in them to make business decisions, initiate sexual relationships or buy furniture. To facilitate commerce and encourage population growth, pubs are distributed liberally around the country. On the whole, British pubs are not very similar to American bars. Pubs tend to be reasonably child-friendly, at least during the day — many of the more rural ones style themselves as family eateries and sometimes have outdoor children's play areas or children's menus. Pubs are social hubs, not so much places to go and get hammered. Getting hammered is just a fringe benefit.

The legal drinking age in the U.K. is eighteen — in reality, the law is not very strictly upheld and many people start drinking long before that. There's some sort of law that says you can drink wine with a meal when you're sixteen, and only when accompanied by someone twice your age with grey hair, or some such. Anyway, it doesn't matter much because if you look much more than sixteen you're unlikely ever to be asked for ID in a pub, unless that pub was formerly a hotbed of under-age drinking and has been threatened with closure several times.

Pubs

You will never get table service in a pub for drinks. Well, let's not say never. You will get table service in the occasional snooty London wine bar. Suffice to say that if you don't look at the drinks menu and think, "are these prices for bottles or glasses?" then you're not getting table service. You're also unlikely to find a drinks menu on your table —to find out which drinks they have you generally need to go to the bar and look at the beer taps. They may also have some sort of board on the wall showing beer and wine. On the up side you will never be expected to tip for drinks. Don't even try it — they won't know what's going on. If you're desperate to ask the bartender for a date or apologise for the vomit they're going to discover in a urinal shortly, the best way to tip them is to offer to buy them a drink. In city bars this will probably just result in them chalking one up in the till to buy later; in country pubs they'll more than likely drink it there and then.

Once you've decided what you and your party want to drink, someone will have to go to the bar and buy the round.

Rules for Buying Rounds

Brits always buy drinks in rounds. Even if they're with people they don't know, they will buy drinks in rounds. This system, whilst clearly open to abuse, has worked for several hundred years due to a tacit agreement by the entire population concerning certain rules. If drinking with Brits, you must adhere to these rules.

Beer is to be bought in pints only. Do not buy a half-pint of beer (unless you are a woman) or a bottle of beer (which are reserved for nancy-boys and Londoners). Drivers or people who are clearly already drunk will occasionally be permitted half-pints. Spirits are for women only when served with mixers.

Do not try to pay anyone back for a round of drinks. Even if there is not a chance in hell of you having another one that night, you shouldn't feel guilty about not being able to get a round in. On most evenings, someone will end up slightly out of pocket. Perhaps you'll be with the same people drinking every night; perhaps the guy who just bought two rounds in a row will be someone you never see again. The assumption is that over a lifetime these will balance out such that nobody really ends up out of pocket. Don't feel bad about accepting drinks from strangers, and don't feel bad about buying them. Of course, there will always be people who are unusually extravagant with rounds and there will be people who are somewhat miserly — the former tend to be regarded as a little showy, and the latter will find themselves out of drinking buddies within a fairly short space of time.

Do not try to opt out of the system. The only valid reason anyone may opt out of buying rounds is if they're driving. Even then, they may be required to nominally take part in the system with an unwritten agreement that their round won't come up as often as anyone else's. If you're intending only having one drink for reasons other than driving (a practice known in the U.K. as "being a poof") then you must still buy rounds for everyone else. This is your penalty for not drinking. Don't moan and whine about it, as the minute you've buggered off home the entire conversation will be about what a boring git you are, and tight-fisted to boot.

Never offer to pay if someone else goes to the bar. Even if you can find a willing co-conspirator, this sort of behaviour is bang out of order. No matter how rich you are, an important part of buying a round involves trying to remember the drinks everyone wanted, squeezing your way to the bar, shouting vainly at the barman, collecting your dripping-wet change, trying to squeeze in between the barflies to collect your drinks and then attempting to carry six beers back to the table via some ferrying system without crashing into anyone and without spilling them.

Some Tips

Once you are familiar with the rules, you might find these tips useful.

The first round is a good one to buy. There's a good chance you're all standing around the bar, so you won't have to carry fourteen drinks across the place, and whilst everyone will remember who bought the first round it's a little debatable as to who will recall who bought the fifth.

If you have more beers to buy than you possess arms, it's permissible to ask your friends for some help in carrying beers back to the table. However it is also permissible for your friends to simply ignore this request, in which case you'll have to make several trips back and forth to bring them to the table. The request should be phrased in such a way as to give someone the opportunity to volunteer, rather than make anyone feel obliged: "Any of you fuckers want to give me a hand?" or some such. An alternate tactic is to try to signal from the bar that the drinks are ready and perhaps someone would like to come and grab a couple of them. Often this will elicit a more favourable response as it doesn't involve any waiting around and will enable your volunteer to speed up the delivery of his own beer.

You will get Manly Kudos for carrying three pints of beer at once. Note that Manly Kudos in the U.K. accrues in a silent fashion, and is not accompanied by whooping or cheering. Carrying four beers at once will normally cause some nods of appreciation. These are the British equivalent of taking your shirt off and running around the bar, punching the air and shouting "U-S-A! U-S-A!" If four beers are carried by a tourist, they will be talked about for decades afterwards by the local barflies.

The easiest way to carry four beers is to grasp one in each hand between your thumb and index finger, and then piggy-back a second one further away from you between your index finger and middle finger. The remaining fingers can be curled under the second glass to provide some vertical support. It's impossible to actually pick up two beers in one hand like this. Carrying four pints in such a fashion is only made possible by the fact that you can grasp two in each hand and then push the four glasses together in order to lift the set. The stability of the finished structure is reliant on glass-on-glass friction which, although stronger than one might expect, is still very near zero. Once lifted from the bar the entire configuration is a volatile one — any large slippage between the glasses horizontally or vertically will likely lead to catastrophe. As a certain amount of slippage will normally occur in transit, you may find that you have to enlist some helpers to dismantle the structure upon arrival. You will likely find a number of willing volunteers, not only because they yearn for some vicarious glory but also because if they don't help you're likely to throw half a gallon of beer over the assembled party and probably cause their ejection from the drinking establishment. Helpers will often stand up. This is because they only have one change of clothes with them.

Do not buy a round of drinks with a credit card. Whilst credit card transactions are the norm in bars in the U.S., they are not in the U.K. If they are even able to take credit cards (which in rural pubs is almost guaranteed not to be the case), the transaction will probably involve the bar-person tut-tutting and then going into the back room to try and find the credit card machine. As they fumble around under the bar looking for a pen, all the other customers will glare at you like a love child at a funeral.

Service is an art. Customers waiting at the bar are rarely served in the order in which they arrived. The most reliable method for being served promptly is to stand close to the bar (perhaps leaning gently on it, but not right over it) and smile as often as possible at a barperson of your choice. Things that will get you served faster than average are:

- Being attractive, and of the opposite sex to the bar person
- Being tall
- Knowing the bar person

Things that will get you served slower than average are:

- Shouting or whistling
- Waving money
- Leaning right over the bar
- Being noticeably drunk (unless also attractive, in which case this may be a positive feature)
- Being small
- Being clearly a part of an enormous group and therefore about to try and buy seventeen drinks, a third of which you've forgotten already and another third of which you're going to have to shout back to your friends to find out what they want
- Being English (in Scotland)
- Being Scottish (in England)

- Being French (universal)

The key to drinking in the U.K. is really just accepting it as substantially different to drinking in the U.S. There's a lot more waiting around. Customer service is quite simply not something that's involved in the process. You'll no doubt drip beer all down your second-best suit whilst trying to carry the three goddamned beers you just paid for back to some bunch of idiots that you only just met. But hey, no tips! And as time goes on, you will develop a warm, comfortable feeling about people in general — sure, you just bought a drink for that guy with the funny hair who turned out not to be your colleague's boyfriend after all. But some day, from someone, you'll get it back. Maybe you'll even fall in love and stuff.

TELLING THE TIME

In Britain, there are only fifty-five minutes in an hour. This means that the day is 8% shorter, and so as time goes on, the day tends to slip a little when compared with the position of the sun. By the end of a month, people find that they're getting up for work just as the sunset is finishing. In order to remedy this, a "leap day" is inserted into every second month or so – the specific months are chosen by the Queen in a televised royal proclamation. The ceremony, reminiscent of the historic "changing of the guard," takes place at Buckingham Palace, the Queen's official residence in London. The current holder of the ceremonial House of Commons position "Black Rod" approaches the Queen's residence carrying the Mace, an ornamental staff normally kept in the Parliament. Watches in silence from behind a cordon by hordes of tourists, he knocks three times sharply on the Queen's front door. The Queen emerges, often wearing her nightgown, shuffles around a little peering at the ground and shortly declares in a loud voice whether or not she is able to see her shadow. If she can see her shadow, a leap day is added to the current month oh, no, it's no good; I just can't keep this up. Back to why telling the time in Britain is different.

Brits use a variety of terms which are unfamiliar to Americans, and vice versa. Brits do not say "a quarter of three," like Americans do. Examples of times you may hear used are:

- "half three" (3:30)
- "ten after two" (2:10)
- "midday" (exactly noon, not some time around lunchtime)

Like all Europeans they use the 24hr clock a lot more than Americans do – almost all written times will be in the 24hr clock, but only in the military will you see people agreeing to meet at "fifteen hundred hours" – in conversation Brits will not say "fifteen o'clock," and will instead revert to the AM/PM system.

It is a popular American misconception that "GMT" means "the time in Britain." It does not. During the winter, Britain does indeed match GMT but in the summer she switches to "British Summer Time" (BST), which is an hour ahead of GMT.

THE BRITISH EDUCATION SYSTEM

Contrary to popular belief, there is an education system in the United Kingdom. Even in Wales. Whilst the curriculum is broadly very similar to most, there's a selection of terminology which isn't. First off, "school" in the U.K. is never used to describe higher education institutions.

Public Schools

The term "public school" is something of a confusing one. In the U.S., somewhat reasonably, this applies to schools supported by the state. In the U.K., these are known as "state schools." The term "public school" is used in England and Wales (not as much in Scotland) to describe the more expensive of the private schools.

The curious name arose in the days before state-funded education, when public schools were open to anyone (with cash) whilst the "private" schools were run by guilds or churches and as such only available for the children of people belonging to a particular profession or religion.

Stages and Exams

I don't want to write too much about this, partly because I'm lazy and partly because the exam system seems to change every year. Schooling in the U.K. is broken into two segments, much the same as the U.S. Children arrive at school at the age of five or six, and are in "primary school" until the age of around eleven. They then move to "senior school" (usually this will be another school entirely, but some schools feature a combined junior and senior school) and stay there until they are around sixteen. Here ends the compulsory education required for all children. To go to university, kids will usually stay on at the same school past the age of sixteen into an extra year or two (a "sixth form" department) during which they sit the exams they need for university.

Regional Variations

The Scottish exam system is not the same as the English one. It's pretty similar, but different enough that both Scotland and England think theirs is secretly superior. They differ in fairly dull ways that I now can't be bothered trying to enumerate.

GETTING AROUND

Street Layout

European streets on the whole are not laid out very sensibly. There are several downsides to having quaint, rustic old buildings dotted around the town centre. One of them is that when they were built they were often in the middle of a vast space of land that is now covered in other buildings. The streets that weave between these great old buildings therefore wind around the place in a somewhat unpredictable fashion, and have over time become larger in order to accommodate motor traffic. The end result of this tends to be a city centre "with character." A city centre with character means one in which a drunk tourist will rarely be able to find his hotel without hailing a taxi.

American streets run north–south, and east–west. If you can stomach the somewhat dull cityscape this creates, this is a great idea. European streets do not follow this logic. As a result, Americans are born with an ingrained notion of which direction they are facing. Europeans are not. Europeans would find an American sign that said "no parking north of here" as confusing as a sign that read "no parking nearer Dave's house than here." Americans often use numbered streets in one direction, and named streets in the other. This is also an excellent idea, but would be a waste of time for Europeans, as no street runs particularly in any constant direction. Americans streets are split into blocks of approximately equal sizes. European streets are not.

I think the difference in town planning is best illustrated by an example of each. Here's an American tourist asking for directions in New York:

Tourist: *Hello there!*

Local: *Not interested, buddy.*

Tourist: *Uh, I just need directions, man.*

Local: *Oh sorry, I thought you were asking for money.*

Tourist: *Jesus! What is wrong with people these days?*

Local: *Where d'you want to go? I'm in a hurry.*

Tourist: *Can you tell me how to get to Whole Foods?*

Local: *Sure. Go north about five blocks, then east onto Madison. It's two or three blocks down on the right.*

And now let's look at a British tourist asking for directions in London.

Tourist: *Hello there!*

Local: *Not interested, mate.*

Tourist: *Erm, hello! I wonder if I can ask you for directions?*

Local: *Oh sorry, I thought you were scrounging.*

Tourist: *Goodness me, what has the world come to?*

Local: *Where d'you want to go? I'm in a hurry.*

Tourist: *I wonder if you could tell me the way to Marks and Spencer?*

Local: *It's just by the Bush Monument.*

Tourist: *Hmm...I'm afraid I don't know where that is, I'm just on holiday here.*

Local: *Crumbs...well, if you head down to the river, then —*

Tourist: *Where's the river?*

Local: *It's just down past the Fox and Hounds on the one-way cobbled bit.*

Tourist: *Which direction?*

Local: *Over there. Well, you can't see it very easily for those trees.*

Tourist: *But there's a car park over there.*

Local: *The road sort of curves to the left around the car park, then goes around this corner with a fork in it — the left fork just goes into a housing estate but the right one goes towards the Fox and Hounds.*

Tourist: *So just straight down there?*

Local: *Yeah, until you see a McDonald's. Or is it a Burger King. Then you turn right at the next light.*

Tourist: *I turn after the McDonald's or just when I see it?*

Local: *Are you sure you don't know the Bush Monument?*

Tourist: *Yes, I'm positive, I only arrived this morning.*

Local: *OK, well, the river is just after that turning. You might want to write this down, to be honest.*

Tourist: *No, no, it's fine; I'll remember it.*

Local: *Well once you hit the river you'll want to head towards the mosque. Don't cross the river.*

Tourist: *What mosque?*

Local: *The mosque! I don't know how to describe it. It's a mosque. It'll be perfectly obvious.*

Tourist: *It'll be ahead of me when I reach the river?*

Local: *Well, sort of. There's a cobbled bit as you get down to the river itself. You might have to try and see the mosque earlier if you can.*

Tourist: *OK thank you ... and then I'll get to the Bush Monument?*

Local: *No. They didn't put the Bush Monument very near the mosque.*

[Tourist and local laugh heartily]

Local: *Basically head for the mosque until you see Cardinal Street. In fact, now I think about it, those general instructions work fine from here too. Head for the mosque until you see Cardinal Street. Except the river's in the way, obviously.*

Tourist: *Splendid — and the Bush Monument is on Cardinal Street?*

Local: *It's right there; you couldn't miss it.*

Tourist: *Thank you very much.*

Local: *To be honest if I was you I might get a minicab.*

Tourist: *Is there a minicab office near here?*

Local: *There's one by the old dental hospital.*

Inside Buildings

The terminology for floor numbering is different between the U.K. and the U.S. In the U.K. (and on the European continent), the first level of a building is called the "ground floor" — the one on the ground. The next one up is the first floor. In the U.S., the level you walk into off the street is the first floor.

This conjures up the image of an American high-powered executive, hungry and listless, trapped forever on the first floor of a British office looking for the exit. Well, it does for me. Some new American buildings are adopting the British floor-numbering system, renaming the first floor "ground" but keeping the second one as "2." I have to admit (I'm not putting it in writing, mind) that I thought the Americans had the right idea here originally.

My wild conjecture as to how this might have ended up happening is that it stems from a time when buildings only had one floor and nobody ever thought about what to label further floors. When one of the smarter peasants in the village discovered that he could extend his hut upwards, he perhaps labelled his new addition the "first floor" to denote that it was the first extra floor, on top of the existing one that all buildings clearly have to have. All of the other peasants were even more impressed when he installed the world's first elevator, and just went along with his naming scheme for the buttons even if they didn't think it made a heap of sense. He was very much the golden boy of the dark ages, and as such people would probably have been burned for saying anything uncomplimentary about him.

He died penniless, as there was no money then.

DRIVING

The Brits drive on the left side of the road, in right-hand-drive cars. In actual fact a surprising amount of the rest of the world drives on the other side of the road – 34% by population, and 28% by length of road system. The notable right-hand drive areas are the U.K., Japan, India, parts of Africa, bits of the Caribbean, some chunks of South East Asia and all of Australasia. The only RHD country with a large number of LHD borders (all of them, in fact) is Thailand. The only way to get out of Thailand in a car is via a complex system of jump ramps with clearly posted minimum and maximum approach speeds.

Although horror stories abound, driving in the U.K. just requires a bit of concentration rather than a vast change of mindset. Especially for the first ten minutes. I've tried to separate the following sections by importance – if you are driving whilst reading this, the first one will suffice.

Very Important Things

Drive on the left. When in busy traffic this is remarkably easy to remember, but you also have to do it whilst exiting quiet side roads, or inside a supermarket car park.

Turn left onto roundabouts. British roundabouts work the same as the small number of them that exist in the U.S. (priority is given to those on the roundabout), but they go clockwise. Usually there are big blue arrows to remind you.

Never turn on red, even if there's nobody anywhere near. In Europe, turning on red isn't any different to just blowing a red light.

Cars and pedestrians never have a "go" signal at the same time. Cars behind you will not be expecting you to stop for pedestrians whilst turning right.

Do stop for people at pedestrian crossings, which are lines across the road much like U.S. pedestrian crossings. I say "much like," but actually they're probably identical. Perhaps the American ones are wider to better accommodate a fuller-figured population.

Quite Important Things

On multi-lane roads, the right lanes really are passing lanes in the U.K. If you are caught passing someone on the left it's a "dangerous driving" conviction. Even if there's nobody behind you, you should stay over in the left lane. There are no carpool lanes. There are bus lanes – some of them are full-time; some of them have signs saying when they're operational. Some buses have cameras attached to them to catch you driving in their lanes.

Speed camera

The Brits have speed cameras. They catch you after you've gone past, so as you're coming up on them they just look like a big box on a stick. Speed cameras in England are painted orange – this was because of an unfortunate legal case where the police claimed they weren't simply revenue generators, and were actually placed at accident black-spots in order to slow motorists down to a safer speed. If that were so, went the court case, then they should make them more obvious.

Make sure your passenger is well-trained in looking out for speed cameras, and that you have an established system of screaming and waving when one is sighted. If you are caught by a speed camera you will see two bright flashes half a second or so apart – the system is entirely automatic and so a citation will appear through the mail in due time. If you're driving a rental car, it will appear on the doorstep of your rental company who normally have a well-oiled system for ensuring its successful delivery to your home address. It is the responsibility of the car owner to name the driver who was in the car at the time – this at least allows you the luxury of spreading the accrued penalty points throughout your immediate family or employees.

The cameras pointing towards you are for the traffic coming the other way, and can't catch you, even if they flash.

Etiquette

In the U.K., flashing your headlights always means "go ahead," and people do it a great deal. If you're letting someone into your lane they may not actually move until you flash the lights. Likewise for letting attractive women out at junctions, merging onto motorways, et cetera.

The fact that everyone is supposed to stay in the slow lane all the time serves to make merging something of a lottery. If you're coming in from an on-ramp, people don't tend to make a lot of room for you and sometimes you actually find yourself having to stop at the end of the ramp.

If you're pulling into a two-lane road from a side road, Brits tend to wait for both lanes to be clear, rather than just the closest one (bear in mind that everyone will generally be in that lane).

Drink-Driving

Drink-driving is not as common in the U.K. as it is in the U.S., and people are pulled over more often. The police don't need to have any reason to pull you over, so they will often just pick up random vehicles and breathalyse the drivers (field sobriety tests are not used in the U.K.). As in most places, the further you get into the country the more likely you are to get away with drink driving.

Speeding

30mph Speed Limit

The Brits measure in miles - the speed limit is 30 mph in town (the sort of places where there would be a 25/35 limit in the U.S.), 60 mph on single-carriageway roads and 70 mph on dual-carriageway roads. Normally the speed limits are denoted by round red-rimmed signs with numbers in them, but most of the 70 mph limits are instead denoted by a "national speed limit applies" sign, which is a white circle with a black line through it. This was presumably done in order to make the motorway limit an easy one to change, although in reality it's never changed since its inception in 1965.

"National Speed Limit Applies"

The speed limit on single carriageway roads without lighting (most country roads) is 60 mph. For some roads this seems very fast indeed, and the limit technically applies even to roads so narrow that they can only permit one car down them at a time and have "passing places" to allow passing. Driving down these roads at 60 mph is great fun, but whilst you may not be breaking the speed limit you may still be collared for "driving too fast for the conditions." In reality, though, you are much more likely to get caught speeding in heavily populated areas or motorways. Funds collecting from speeding fines do not go into regional county coffers in the U.K., and as such they tend not to be quite so devious about finding offenders.

There are some 40 or 50 mph limits around the place but they're clearly signed. Most of the speed cameras are in 30 mph or 40 mph areas but there are a couple on the nice fast 60 mph roads. There are currently none on motorways, but there are a lot more police cars on motorways so it's best not to go much above 85 mph.

Cheap Fuel

After some driving around the place you're eventually going to have to fill up with fuel. At this point you've probably been in the U.K. for a day or two, and therefore have heard Brits whimpering on and on about how expensive petrol is. You may be surprised, therefore, to note as you pull into the petrol station that fuel appears to be significantly cheaper than it is in the U.S. Goddamned Brits. All they do is moan about things constantly. And why does it rain all the time? You should have listened to your boss and gone to Italy after all. At least they have edible food. As you squeeze the pump handle and watch the numbers fly, you will quickly realise that in the U.K. fuel is priced by the litre, and not by the gallon at all. There are roughly four litres in a U.S. gallon.

DICTIONARY

Call me conventional, but I've chosen to arrange the following sections in alphabetical order.

Although it may occasionally appear not to be the case, there is a format to this portion. Each word is in bold, followed immediately by as succinct a definition as I can think up. I am permitting myself to use American English in the succinct definition portions, but other than that I'm using British English throughout. If there is more than one definition, I've preceded each one by a number. Occasionally a word has a meaning specific to Britain but also another meaning shared by both Brits and Americans – in these cases I've added that international definition next to the British one and written "(universal)" after it. I probably haven't done this in all cases, only in the ones where you might have been confused. And only in the ones I remembered to go back and fix.

Words in italics are words which are foreign to an American reader – they are usually British English, but occasionally in etymologies they're from other languages entirely.

Where I thought pronunciations weren't obvious, I've added them. I deviated from my dictionary style here and wrote the pronunciations in a format that a twelve-year old would understand, and not the hieroglyphics that dictionaries like to use. Words in italics are other British words defined elsewhere.

A note – there are not that many words in this dictionary. Many others contain more words. This is not because I'm lazy. This is because I've tried to only include words which the eager tourist may use in everyday speech with the reaction of "ooh, what a multi-cultured person" rather than "what in the name of god does that mean." The words in this dictionary are ones that people use in everyday life, not ones that they only wheel out to impress or confuse foreigners.

The fact that I'm lazy is a coincidence.

A

abseil *v* dangle oneself from a cliff at the end of a rope. In the U.S. military, *abseil* is used to distinguish face-out dangling from the more conventional face-in rappelling, but civilian Americans know the whole dangling business as "rappeling." The word is apparently derived from the German *abseilen*, meaning simply "to rope down." Those crazy Germans and their crazy language.

aerial *n* bent bit of wire intended to collect radio waves for your computer, television or some such device. The manufacturers don't call them bent bits of wire. Their marketing chaps have many fancy words like "impedance" and "gain," but back at the factory all the guys are just bending wire. Americans call these devices "antennas," though *aerial* is in limited use in the U.S., too.

afters *n* dessert. One would imagine that they're so named because they come after the main meal, but actually they take their name from their inventor, Sir George After, the Fat Bastard of Brighton.

AGA *n* large coal-filled cooking stove not dissimilar to an American "range." AGA is a brand name; the company primarily produces those giant cooking stoves that are filled with coal and the whole of the top

of the thing gets very hot indeed. They're a bit dated now, but pretty much everyone's granny had one.

agony aunt *n* advice columnist – a newspaper or magazine employee who responds publicly to readers' impassioned pleas for help on a wide range of issues, but most commonly sex. Read by a large sector of the population, each of whom hopes to find a vicarious solution to their own dark sexual inadequacies.

alight *v* disembark. Many American tourists are confronted with this word quite rapidly after reaching the U.K., because on the London Underground the pre-recorded message says such things as: "This is Baker Street. Alight here for Madame Tussauds." Madame Tussauds is a cheesy attraction and best avoided. The voice on the tube only says the part about the alighting.

aluminium (al-yoo-min-i-um) *n* aluminum. Who is correct about this one is a matter for some debate. We can at least say that Hans Ørsted, the Danish gentleman who discovered it in 1824, had based its name on the Latin word "alumus," denoting the mineral alum. The difference in spelling seems to have originated when very early printed material advertising his talks on the subject contained the two different spellings in error. The general consensus seems to be that he had originally intended using the "British" spelling (borne out by International Union of Pure and Applied Chemistry's use of it, and the "ium" suffix that already graced many metallic elements at the time), but as he clearly didn't make any efforts to correct anyone, we could conclude that he didn't care too much either way. The American scientific community use the British spelling.

anorak 1 *n* someone who's a little bit too knowledgeable about one subject. Generally a subject like seventeenth-century flower pots or steam trains, rather than athletic sexual positions or gun-fighting. Americans (and also Brits, as our languages merge ever closer) would call such a person a "geek." It may originate with the fans of Radio Caroline, a U.K. offshore pirate radio station, whose fans had to don anoraks in order to visit the station. **2** *n* waterproof jacket (universal).

answerphone *n* device plugged into the telephone which answers it for you when you're out, playing an oh-so-hilarious message that you got from the internet, recorded from Seinfeld or made up yourself whilst plastered and forgot about. Americans call them "answering machines," which has become more common than "answerphone" in the U.K. nowadays.

anti-clockwise *adv* rotation in a direction which isn't clockwise (as, well, the phrase suggests). Americans will know this better as "counter-clockwise." Of course, anyone with half a brain could have worked this out themselves but never let it be said that we're only paying lip-service to completeness.

anyroad *adv* very much an equivalent of "anyway." If you think about it, "any road" pretty much means "any way," erm, anyway.

arse *n* **1** what you sit on. Very close in meaning to the American "ass," although actually derived from a different root, as *arse* is an old English word meaning "tail." **I can't be arsed** I can't be bothered. **bunch of arse** load of nonsense: *I never bothered reading the bible, the whole thing is a bunch of arse.* **2** *interj* rats. Used alone in a similar fashion to *bollocks*: *I'm sorry to tell you, sir, but you've missed the last train. / Arse!*

arsehole *n* asshole.

artic *n* *abbr* articulated vehicle, usually a large hauling truck or semi.

articulated lorry *adj* semi truck which is able to bend in the middle. Of course, I just wrote pretty much the same thing two seconds ago. I'm beginning to understand why the guy who wrote the first Oxford English Dictionary ended up going mad and cutting his penis off.

aubergine *n* large purple pear-shaped vegetable North Americans will recognise as "eggplant."

autumn *n* season between summer and winter. Americans call it "fall." Americans, of course, also call it "autumn" which might have you wondering why it's in here at all. Well, my furry friend, it is in here because Brits never call it "fall." Think of this entry not so much as "autumn," but more as "not fall."

B

bagsie *v* stake a claim for something in the same way that Americans would claim "dibbs" on or "call" some item or privilege: *I bagsie the front seat* or *Bagsie first shot on the dodgems!* It's a rather childlike sentiment; you would be less likely to hear *I bagsie being Financial Director!* It doesn't seem ridiculously far-fetched that it'd be derived from "bags I," with "bag" meaning to catch something. But hey, who can tell. [Etymologists. – *ed.*]

bairn *n Scottish* baby. Possibly derived from the old Norse word "barn," which means both "child" and "children."

baked potato *n* potato. Baked. You can buy a baked potato on either side of the pond, of course, but in the U.K. you will specify the filling as you buy the baked potato, while in the U.S. you'll be brought a small selection of fillings to plonk in yourself. British fillings tend to constitute more of a whole meal than American ones.

Baltic *n* very cold: *I'm not going outside without a coat, it's bloody Baltic!* Presumably named for the Baltic states, which aren't all that cold.

bangers *n* sausages. Probably most often heard in the name of the dish "bangers and mash" (the "mash"

being mashed potato, but I hope to God you worked that out yourself). So called because they make popping noises when you cook them.

bank holiday *n* any public holiday for which the public have forgotten the original purpose. You know, that holiday on the fourth Wednesday in June. It was something to do with Saint Swithen, I think. He was born maybe. Or was he beheaded?

bap *n* **1** small bread roll. **2** woman's breast (modern slang): *Get your baps out, love!*

barmpot *n* clumsy idiot. As with a lot of the Brits' less-than-complimentary words, it isn't really offensive — it's used more in goading fun than anything else. Has a derivation similar to that of "barmy."

barmy *adj* idiotic. You might describe your father's plan to pioneer the first civilian moon landing using nothing but stuff he'd collected from a junkyard as "barmy." Well, unless the junkyard he had in mind was out the back of Cape Kennedy and he had funding from China. It may or may not derive from the fact that there was once a psychiatric hospital in a place called Barming, near Maidstone in Kent, England. It may equally easily come from an Old English word for yeast, "barm," intended to imply that the brain is fermenting. As these competing etymologies seem equally plausible, it seems only sensible to settle the matter in an old-fashioned fistfight.

barnet *n* hair; hairstyle. Another example of Cockney rhyming slang which has slipped into the common vernacular: "Barnet Fair" / "hair." Barnet is an area of London. Presumably they had a fair there at some point.

barney *n* argument; fight. This is certainly rhyming slang, but no one's sure of whence it came. It could either be "Barney Rubble" / "trouble" (Barney Rubble is a character in the cartoon "The Flintstones"), or "Barn Owl" / "row" (when it means "fight," "row" rhymes with "now"). The latter is marginally more likely, as "trouble" could be many things other than a fight, but the former is a more popular explanation. Pick one.

barrister *n* sort of lawyer. Barristers are different from solicitors in such a convoluted way it took a barrister a whole page of ball-bouncingly dull prose to explain it to me.

bash on *interj* press on regardless, to keep struggling in the face of adversity. Has nothing to do with hitting people.

beavering *v* working enthusiastically. These days you'd have difficulty saying it without a chorus of sniggers from the peanut gallery, as everyone in the U.K. is well aware of the American use of the word "beaver." It's the sort of thing your grandmother might say at Christmas dinner that would make the younger generations choke on their soup.

Belisha Beacons *n* yellow flashing lights on sticks that are positioned next to zebra crossings and flash constantly to alert drivers. They were named after Hore Belisha, who was Minister of Transport when they were introduced. Perhaps a more interesting derivation was put forward by an episode of the BBC radio programme "Radio Active," which featured an unwinnable quiz, one of the questions being "From where did the Belisha Beacon get its name?" Answer: "From the word 'beacon'." I was younger then, and in the cold light of day it seems less funny now than it once did. You can't take away my childhood.

bell end *n* end of one's nob, which devoid of a foreskin looks not completely unlike a church bell. If you don't have one to examine, ask a friend or neighbour: *I don't know what happened last night but when I woke up this morning my bell end was covered in spots!*

bender *n* **1** big drinking session (universal). **2** homosexual (rather derogatory). Be careful with this one. It possibly derives from the, erm, position classically adopted by male homosexuals. It's a very old term, and predates female homosexuals.

berk *n* idiot. Yes, yes, another friendly U.K. word for moron; this one implies a degree of clumsiness: *Look, you berk, I said to bend it, not bust it.* The word originally derives from the rhyming slang "Berkeley Hunt" (or "Berkshire Hunt"), which rhymes with — well, "punt," among other words.

bespoke *adj* made especially for a particular client's requirements. These days it's most likely to be used to describe computer software, but it could cover anything from limousines to suits. Americans would probably say "tailor made" or "customized."

bevvy *n* alcoholic drink. A contraction of "beverage."

big end *n* the end of the conrod, which is attached to the crankshaft in a conventional combustion engine. The other end, attached to the piston, is called the "small end."

Bill *n* the police, in the same sort of a way as "Plod." There are two possible etymologies: The first, that it's after William Wilberforce, a Member of Parliament who first proposed a U.K. police service. The second, that all police cars originally had the letters "BYL" in their number plates. *The Bill* is also a popular U.K. television drama about a police station.

billion *n* thousand million. As you may have noticed, this is precisely the same as the U.S. definition. It's here because some time ago in the U.K. it meant a million million, which no doubt caused a lot of confusion.

Billy no-mates *n* person with no friends: *Everyone else turned up half an hour late so I was sitting there like Billy no-mates for ages.*

bin *n* trashcan. This is simply a contraction of "dustbin" (which means the same thing, to save you going and looking it up). **wheelie bin** a *bin* on wheels. Normally refers to *bins* provided and emptied by the local council. **bin bags** garbage bags. The plastic bags one puts in the *bin*.

bint *n* woman, in the loosest sense of the word. One step short of a prostitute, a *bint* is a bird with less class, less selectivity, more makeup and even more skin. Blokes don't talk to bints unless they've had at least eight pints of beer, which is why bints turn up in free-for-students nightclubs at 2:45 a.m. with their faked student ID and dance around their Moschino rucksacks. The word derives from the Arabic for "woman." Well, I say "derives from" – it *is* the Arabic for "woman."

bird *pron. "beud" (London); "burd" (Scotland) n* woman. Well, not really. *Bird* is used by blokes looking upon the fairer sex with a slightly more carnal eye. It's not quite at the stage of treating women as objects but the implication is certainly there: *I shagged some random bird last night* (a popular usage), or: *Hey, Andy, I think those birds over there are looking at us.* You'd never describe your grandmother as a bird. It's popular in Scotland to refer to one's girlfriend as "ma burd" — but do it in front of her and you'll be choking teeth. About the only thing worse would be to call her "ma bint," which will warrant a foot in the testicles and a loose tongue concerning your sexual prowess. The word itself is derived from the Old Norse word for "woman," and the closest American English equivalent would probably be "chick."

Biro *n* ball-point pen. Named after Hungarian journalist Ladislo Biro, who invented it. It's slipped into the common vernacular in the U.K. and the rest of Europe as a generic word for a ball-point pen.

biscuit *n* cookie. Has nothing to do with what Americans call a biscuit.

bitter *n* proper beer, made with hops and served at room temperature (not actually warmed, contrary to popular opinion). The European/American fizzy lager shite is not real beer.

blag *v* wheedle; bluff; wangle: *I managed to blag a ride to work.* Or: *I had no idea what I was talking about but I think I managed to blag it.* Perhaps if I sat for a bit longer I'd think up better examples. Likely derived from the French "blague," meaning a tall story. Americans use "mooch" and "moocher" in the same context.

bleeding *adj* similar to "bloody." Used extensively by Cockneys (i.e., in London). Consequently, there are no recorded incidents of the trailing "g" being enunciated.

blighter *adj* guy (or, rather, a more refined, more upper-class version thereof). Usually used in a slightly critical tone: *Just wait until I get my hands on the blighter who*

steals my newspaper every morning.

Blighty *n* Britain. A very antiquated term itself and seen most often these days in war films: *Well chaps, I don't mind saying I'll be dashed pleased when we're out of this pickle and back in Blighty.* It is derived from the Urdu word "Bilati" meaning "provincial, removed at some distance" and was one of the many words that slipped into English during Indian colonisation.

blimey *interj* nice mild expletive, in terms of rudeness on a par with "my goodness." It was originally part of the phrase "cor blimey," which was likely a contraction of "God blind me," which was in turn an abbreviated version of "may God blind me if it is not so." There has been little evidence of God blinding users of the word, whether what they were saying was true or not. The original phrase "cor blimey" is still used, but rarely.

blinding *adj* unusually wonderful. A currently popular slang term, largely interchangeable with "brilliant" or "great." You'd use it to describe the goal that your football team just scored, or your favourite Elton John song. Though if you even had a favourite Elton John song, there's a good chance you're unfamiliar with current slang.

blinking *adj* damned. A lesser equivalent to "bloody." Slightly old-fashioned, but still in widespread use.

bloke *n* guy. A bloke is a Joe Public, a random punter — any old fellow off the street. Unlike "guy," however, it can't apply to your friends. You can't walk up to a group of your mates and say "Hi blokes, what's up?" as they'd all peer at you as if you'd been reading some ill-informed, cheap dictionary. Without question, the most common usage of the word is in the phrase "some bloke in the pub."

bloody *adj* **1** damned. An exclamation of surprise, shock or anger, it's one of the great multi-purpose British swear words. Best known as part of the phrase "Bloody hell!" but can also be used in the middle of sentences for emphasis in a similar way to "fucking": *And then he had the cheek to call me a bloody liar!* or even with particular audacity in the middle of words: *Who does she think she is, Cinde-bloody-rella?* Etymology-wise, it's possible that "bloody" has in fact nothing to do with blood and actually a contraction of the Christian phrase "by Our Lady." **2. bloody-minded** obstinate; determined: *If he wasn't going to be so bloody-minded about it we'd have come to a deal ages ago.*

blooming *adj* darned. An extremely innocuous expletive — could be seen as a reduced-strength version of "bloody." Rather antiquated nowadays.

blow off *v* break wind (rather old-fashioned): *My goodness, is that Deardrie cooking breakfast again?*

/ Hmm, no, I think the dog's blown off. Brits do not use the American meaning (to brush off).

blower *n* telephone: *just a second, I'm on the blower.* Yes, it sounds a bit rude. May stem from the days of party telephone lines, where people would blow into the mouthpiece in order to gently remind whoever was using the line that you wanted to too. Alternately, it may originate with the navy, where intra-ship communications operated using a similar system.

bob *n* five-pence piece. Before the U.K.'s currency system was decimalised in 1971 and became simply "pounds and pence," the Brits had "pounds, shillings and pence." Like all crappy Imperial measures there wasn't ten or a hundred of anything in anything and good riddance to the lot of it. In order to work out how to pay for anything you had to be able to divide by sixteen and nine tenths, subtracting room temperature. A "bob" was a shilling, and these days it's still vaguely recognised as meaning five pence. Only vaguely, though.

bobbie *n* police officer. After Robert Peel, who was instrumental in creating the British police force. It's a little antiquated these days.

bobbins *adj* useless junk. While quite recent slang, it's rather charming: *Did your grandmother leave you anything good? / Nope, just a complete load of ancient bobbins.* One possible etymology: that it's from the north of England (particularly the Lancashire and

Manchester areas), which used to be supported largely by cotton mills. As the industrial revolution drew to a close, the mills closed down and the population found itself with a surfeit of largely worthless milling machinery. During that time the phrase "'twas worth nout but bobbins" sprung up; years later we're left only with the last word.

Bob's your uncle *interj* there you have it; ta-da! It's a little antiquated these days but by no means out of use. It carries a cheerful connotation, so you would be more likely to hear: *And then fold it back again, once over itself like that and Bob's your uncle — an origami swan!* rather than: *Just get a hold of the paedophile register and Bob's your uncle!*

bodge 1 *v* make a bit of a haphazard job of something **2** *n* something cobbled together. A "bodger" was originally a craftsman who worked on a green-wood lathe, but this information is of almost no help at all because the word "bodger" still rather implies that such a person was "bodging" something.

boff *v* shag (somewhat posh equivalent).

boffin *n* wonk. Someone who is particularly knowledgeable about his/her subject. It doesn't quite carry the respect implied in "expert" — calling someone a "boffin" suggests that he has body odour and is a virgin. Boffins are invariably male.

bog *n* toilet. More likely to be used as in: *D'ya hear Fat Bob took a*

kicking in the bogs in Scruffy Murphy's? rather than: *I say, Mrs. Bryce-Waldergard, I'm awfully sorry to trouble you but I was wondering if you could point me in the direction of your bog?*

bog standard *n* no frills. The basic version. So your "bog standard" Volkswagen Golf would be one that doesn't have electric windows, power steering or opposable thumbs. Well, nowadays a bog-standard Golf probably does have two thirds of those things. There's no particular reason to believe that the term has anything to do with a toilet (see "bog").

bogie *n pron. "bo-ghee"* booger. The charming little things everyone excavates from their nose now and again but likes to pretend they don't.

bogroll *n* toilet paper. See "bog."

boiler *n* unattractive woman. The word was mentioned in Deborah Curtis' book *Touching from a Distance,* her memoir of life with Ian Curtis of Joy Division. While their marriage was breaking down, Ian was having an affair with a European woman whom the rest of the band supposedly referred to as "the Belgian boiler."

bollard *n* small concrete or metal post generally used to stop cars from driving into certain places. While used only in a nautical context in the U.S., it is accepted universally in the U.K. When not on boats, Americans call them "pylons," which to Brits are the giant metal structures used to hold up national grid electricity wires.

bollocks 1 *n* testicles. The word is in pretty common use in the U.K. and works well as a general "surprise" expletive in a similar way to "bugger." **the dog's bollocks** something particularly good (yes, good): *See that car — it's the dog's bollocks, so it is.* This in turn gives way to copy-cat phrases such as "the pooch's privates" or "the mutt's nuts," which all generally mean the same thing. **bollocking** a big telling-off **2** rubbish: *Well, that's a load of bollocks.* Some additional U.S./U.K. confusion is added by the fact that the words "bollix" and "bollixed" are sometimes used in the U.S. to describe something thrown into confusion or destroyed.

bolshie *adj* rebellious; a bit of an upstart; a force to be reckoned with. Apparently, in Russian, "bolshoi" means "great."

bolt-hole *n* sanctuary; place one runs to when in trouble or wanting to hide. One might hear it used to describe Winston Churchill's country retreat, or some such.

bomb *n* splendid success: *Our party went off like a bomb.*

bonk *v* **1** have sex: *Did you hear that Howard's been bonking his secretary for the last three years?* **2** a clunk or bash (universal).

bonnet *n* hood of a car; the part of a car which covers the engine. Confusion arises in the U.K. when dealing with rear-engined cars; it's difficult to determine whether to call it a bonnet or, as seems perhaps more logical, a boot, on account of it being at the back. The

trials of modern life. To encourage confusion, "hood" is used in the U.K. to describe the convertible top of a convertible car.

bonny *adj Scottish* beautiful. A little antiquated — you'd be much more likely to hear: *Deirdre's new granddaughter is awfully bonny!* than you would: *Bobby's stolen a bonny new shooter — we're going to go out this evening and do the chip shop over.*

boot *n* trunk of a car. The boot of a car is the part you keep your belongings in. So called because it was originally known as a "boot locker" — whether it used to be commonplace to drive in one's socks is anyone's guess.

boozer 1 *n* pub. **2** one who's in the middle of partaking in booze (universal).

bottle *n* nerve. To "lose one's bottle" is to chicken out of something — often just described as "bottling it." It may be derived from Cockney rhyming slang, where "bottle" = "bottle and glass" = "arse." Losing one's bottle appears therefore to refer to losing the contents of one's bowel.

bounder *n* person who is generally no good, a bad egg. It's very old-fashioned — even Rudyard Kipling would probably have used it in jest. One rather dubious etymology is that it was applied pre–Great War to golfers who used new American golf balls (similar to modern golf balls) instead of the more traditional leather-covered ones. They had a more enthusiastic bounce and the use of such balls was not banned by the rules but was considered bad sportsmanship, perhaps even a little underhanded. The term was originally applied to the ball itself, and only later to the user of such a ball.

box 1 *n* item that fits down the front of a bloke's underwear and protects the crown jewels. Americans know it as a "cup," although I suppose in the U.S. such an item is less likely to be protecting the crown jewels and perhaps instead protects "the Bill of Rights" or some such. **2** female genitalia (universal).

Boxing Day *n* holiday that follows Christmas Day (December 26). A public holiday in the U.K., Australia, New Zealand and Canada, and various other countries that the U.K. once owned. More properly known as St. Stephen's Day. Takes its name, rather disappointingly, from the fact that employers used to celebrate it by giving their employees gifts. In boxes. I was going to make something up here but my mind went blank.

braces 1 *n* suspenders. Beware of the cross-definition — in the U.K., "suspenders" are something else entirely (you'll just have to look it up like a man). **2** metal devices used to straighten one's teeth (universal).

brackets *n* parentheses. The things that Americans call "brackets" [these ones], Brits know better as "square brackets."

brew *n* cup of tea: *Would you like a brew?* Northern English but widely understood elsewhere in the U.K.

At a stretch it could refer to coffee, too.

brick *n* dependable person; rock. Someone who will stand tall in the face of adversity. A largely upper-class term, it is hardly in use nowadays.

bricking it *n* shit scared: *He didn't do very well in the interview – we felt a bit sorry for him as he was clearly bricking it.*

brill *adj* popular abbreviation for "brilliant." Well, popular amongst 1980s adolescents.

brilliant *adj* particularly good: *I had a brilliant holiday*; *What a brilliant night out.* It's a little bit childish — you'd be less likely to refer to a "brilliant board meeting" or a "brilliant shag." Also carries the usual other meanings (as "gifted" or "luminescent") in the U.K.

brolly *n* umbrella.

brush *n* broom. Brits use the word "broom" too (they don't talk about witches flying on brushsticks), but not as often.

bubble and squeak 1 *n* dish made from boiled cabbage and sausages. **2** *n* Greek person, usually shortened to "bubble." From Cockney rhyming slang "bubble and squeak" / "Greek": *Did you hear Harry's brother's gone and started dating a bubble?*

bubtion *pron. "bub-shun" n* Scottish baby. Has a cosy, affable connotation. You'd never refer to your baby as a *bubtion* if it had lately been sick on your three-piece suit and drooled in your cornflakes.

bugger 1 *n* jerk. Or substitute any other inoffensive insult ("git" works just as well) **2** *v* sodomise **3 -off**: a friendlier alternative to "fuck off." **4** *interj* "rats." Stand-alone expletive usable in a similar way as "bollocks": *Oh, bugger!*

bum 1 *n* posterior; pretty much the British equivalent of "butt." **2** *v* mooch: *Mind if I bum a ride home?* or perhaps more amusingly: *Can I bum a fag?* What the Americans call "bums" Brits call "tramps."

bumf *n* copious amounts of paperwork or literature: *You would not believe the bloody stack of bumf that came with my new video recorder.* Possibly derived from the army and a contraction of the phrase "bum fodder," i.e., toilet paper.

burgle *v* break into somewhere and nick stuff. Americans have the hilarious word "burglarize," which means the same thing; for all I know, Yanks might refer to the event as burglarization. Or perhaps not.

busk *v* sit in the street playing an instrument and hoping people will give you money. See also "waster."

butcher's *n* look: *Hey, give me a butcher's at that.* 'From Cockney rhyming slang: "butcher's hook" / "look."

butty *n* colloquial name for something sold in a chippy that's served inside a roll or a folded-over piece of bread. It's a bit of a northern English/Scottish thing, and has more recently started being used to cover pretty much any sort of sandwich. The most popular is a chip butty, but you can also buy bacon or fish butties without

seeming strange. Probably derived from the fact that there is usually as much butter as roll.

C

cack *n* shit: *I've cacked myself; the club was okay but the music was cack.* Well known in the U.K. but perhaps not all that widely used.

cack-handed clumsy; ineptly executed. Likely derived from a time when the left hand was used for cleaning one's posterior after movements, and the right hand reserved for anything else. Therefore anything executed with the left hand is perhaps sub-standard. Almost all scatological etymologies are historically false, but they're more amusing than the polite ones. The sad truth of life is that more of our language derived from the Viking term for "baking tray" than some sort of acronym which spelled "FUCK."

camp *adj* effeminate and homosexual. If you have heard of an Englishman (and latterly New Yorker) named Quentin Crisp, he was the very epitome of *camp.* And even if you haven't heard of him, he still was. Americans will say "flaming" or "swishy" to mean much the same thing, though interestingly some Americans do use "campy" to describe old-fashioned or preposterous humour.

camper van *n* motorised caravan in which you can take your entire family for a horrible holiday. Americans call them "R.V.s," but the average European camper is significantly smaller than the average American one. Also, the average European is, of course, smaller than the average American, as proven by statistics.

candy floss *n* cotton candy. The revolting foodstuff one can buy at fairgrounds which resembles a giant blob of fibreglass wrapped around a stick.

car boot sale *n* merry event where people get together in a field and sell the rubbish from their attic, under the secret suspicion that some part of it might turn out to be splendidly valuable. Not entirely dissimilar to a jumble sale. The term stems no doubt from the fact that this is normally carried out using the boot of your car as a headquarters. This sort of nonsense is now largely replaced by eBay, where you can sell the 1950s engraved brass Hitler moustache replica your father was awarded for twenty years' service in the post office without actually having to meet the freak who bought it.

car park *n* parking lot. The large buildings composed of many floors of just parking spaces are called "multi-storey car parks" in the U.K. but "parking garages" in the U.S.

caravan *n* terrible device which attaches to the back of your car and allows you to take your whole family on holiday at minimal expense and with maximum irritability. They're more popular in Europe than they are in the U.S., where they're called "trailers." Be careful not to confuse a touring caravan (which a family will generally keep outside their house and drag behind their normal car somewhere for a few holidays a year) with a static caravan, which is generally deposited once by a truck and left there. Americans call both of these things "trailers," and where a distinction is needed they'll call the touring variants "travel trailers." The devices that Americans call a "fifth wheel" — caravans which attach to a conventional diesel truck — are pretty much non-existent in the U.K. Another caravan variant common to both sides of the Atlantic is the "trailer tent," which is like a caravan except the walls and roof fold out like some sort of ghastly mobile puppet theatre. No doubt you're much less confused now. I could go on about caravans for days.

cardie *n abbr* cardigan. A common abbreviation, at least for anyone who still wears cardigans.

carrier bag *n* shopping bag. Can't think of anything witty.

casual *n Scottish* bad egg, nogoodnik. Pretty close Scottish equivalent to "yob," with the notable exception that *casuals* will actually refer to themselves as such while yobs certainly would not. Dotted around Edinburgh is graffiti advertising the services of the "Craiglockart Casual Squad." Craiglockart isn't one of the worst areas of Edinburgh, so perhaps their modus operandi is to turn up and insult your intelligence, or throw truffles through your windows.

cat's eyes *n* little reflectors mounted in the centre of the road, amid the white lines. When you're driving along at night your headlights reflect in them to show where the road goes. When you're driving like a screaming banshee they gently bounce the car up and down in order to unsettle it, causing you subsequently to lose traction and crash the rented 1.3-litre VW Polo through a fence and into a yard. Everything goes black — your senses are dead but for the faint smell of petrol, and the dim glow of a light coming on in the farmhouse. Somewhere in the distance a big dog barks. As you slowly regain consciousness, you find that you're in a soft bed, surrounded by candles and with a faint whiff of incense drifting on the breeze from the open window. You see a familiar face peering down at you — could it be Stinky Potter, from down by the cottages? Wasn't that corner just about where they found poor old Danny's motorbike? And how does this guy know your name? If you try to run, roll the dice and turn to page seventeen. If you choose to kiss the old man, turn to page twelve.

central reservation *n* median. Far from being a sought-after restaurant booking, this is in fact what Brits call the grassy area in the centre of a motorway which is there to stop you colliding with oncoming traffic quite as easily as you might.

champion *adj Northern England* great; wonderful: *Ooh, those sausages were champion!*

chancer *n* risk-taker, someone who tends to take the kind of chances that involve things on the greyer side of society — the sort of person who buys random domain names in the hope someone will offer them a pile of money for them, or puts all their money on the rank outsider in the 12:45 at Chepstow.

chap *n* upper-crust equivalent of "bloke." Nowadays only really seen in a tongue-in-cheek way or in 1950s Enid Blyton children's books. It would read something along the lines of: *I say chaps, let's go and visit that strange old man with the raincoat at Bog End Cottage and see if he has any more special surprises for us!* Jolly hockeysticks.

charva *n* newish word in the U.K. to describe a range of people much similar to pikeys. From Romany (spoken by the Roma people, i.e. gypsies) for "child." Used in 1960s London to mean "fuck," as evinced by the Derek Raymond *Factory* series of novels.

chat up *v* make conversation with someone of the opposite sex with the intention of endearing yourself to them: *Arthur spent the whole bloody night chatting up some bird in a wig.* **chat up line** an opening gambit intended to attract the opposite sex. Given that opening lines have a near-zero chance of attracting anyone of the opposite sex, it's a popular pastime amongst British women regurgitating the very worst *chat up lines* they've encountered.

chav *n* variant of "charva."

cheeky *adj* risqué; just short of rude. You're being cheeky if you make a joke that you can only just barely get away with without getting into trouble.

cheerio *interj* goodbye. Fairly old-fashioned and light-hearted. Originates from the 1970s, when one of the favourite killing methods of the Welsh mafia was to intravenously inject the victim with breakfast cereal.

cheers *interj* informal substitute for "thank you." Somehow derived from its use as an all-purpose toast.

chemist *n* **1** drugstore; pharmacist. The American term "drugstore" implies to Brits that you could just buy Class A narcotics over the counter. These days it's also acceptable in Britain to call the place a "pharmacy." **2** a person who works with chemicals (universal).

Chesterfield *n* hard, deep-buttoned leather sofa. The sort of thing you could imagine Sherlock Holmes sitting in.

chippy 1 *n* fish-and-chip shop. **2** *n colloq* carpenter. Americans use this word (at least those on the East Coast) to describe a woman of somewhat suboptimal morals; this derives from its original meaning of an Old West saloon prostitute, commonly paid in poker chips. All this is of minimal relevance here, as that meaning isn't used in the U.K.

chipolata *n* small sausage. The term originated in Mexico, but somehow never made it big in the U.S.

chips *n* French fries. However, it's lately been popular to call thin chips "fries" in the U.K, so Brits at least know what "fries" are these days. Classic chips can be obtained from a chip shop ("chippy") and are a great deal unhealthier. They also vary quite creatively — if you buy them at 9 p.m. they are hard, black and crunchy (because they've been cooking since 6:30 p.m., when the dinner rush came through) but if you buy them at 3 a.m. you will find them very akin to raw potatoes, right down to the green bits in the middle (because the chippy employees want all of these drunk punters out of the door so they can go home).

chivvy on *v* hurry someone along with something. If you want an example, you can have this: *I was pretty sure I'd be up until 1 a.m. daydreaming instead of doing my homework, but my mum chivvied me on with it and I was done fairly early.*

chock-a-block *adj* closely packed together. You might use this to describe your dating schedule or your attic, unless you are unforgivably ugly and you live in a flat, in which case you'd have to

think up something else to use it on. The examples here are provided as-is, you know; they don't necessarily work for everyone. It's possible that the word has a quite unfortunate origin — it may have originally referred to the area where black slaves were once lined up on blocks to be sold. It's also possible that it stems from maritime usage, referring to when a block and tackle were jammed against each other to stop the load moving.

chocolate drops *n* chocolate chips. The idea of "chocolate chips" is enough to turn most British stomachs. The American candy called a "chocolate drop," but it doesn't have a lot to do with British chocolate drops.

Christmas cracker *n* (ah, how to describe these...) bit of fancily-coloured paper wrapped much like a lozenge, with twisted ends. A small sort of explosive device is put inside a cracker so that when two people pull at alternate ends, the whole thing comes apart with a snapping noise and — ah, the joy — a small piece of trinket crap falls out. This will be something like an ineffectual miniature sewing kit, a set of blunt nail clippers or one of these mysterious "get the bits of metal apart" puzzles, which will cause some degree of interest from the surrounding family until someone realises it's very easy to get them apart because it was made in China and came out of the factory bent. As the name suggests, these are mainly used at Christmas but sometimes pop up at birthday parties and the like.

chuff 1 *v* fart. **2** *n* one's posterior. **3** *n* *Northern England* vagina. **4** *interj* general swear word usable much the same as "fuck": *It was all going fine until the chuffing pigs turned up.* Entirely separate from the word "chuffed," so use with care.

chuffed *adj* generally happy with life. You can also get away with saying you are "unchuffed" or "dischuffed" if something gets your back up. Make sure you only use this word in the correct tense and familiarise yourself with the meaning of the word "chuff," too (see previous entry).

cider *n* alcoholic apple juice. To Brits all cider is alcoholic — there's no such thing as "hard cider" in Britain, and any non-alcoholic apple juice is called simply "apple juice."

clap *n* applaud. In the U.K., to "give someone a clap" means to applaud them. Analogous to U.S. English's "give someone a hand." Not to be confused with giving someone "the clap," which means the same thing on both sides of the Atlantic.

clobber *n* clothing; vestments. You might hear: *OK, OK, I'll be out in two minutes once I've got my nightclubbing clobber on.* It's possible this definition is of Scottish origin. Brits do also use "clobber" to mean hitting something.

close *n pron. as in "close to me," rather than "close the door"* residential street with no through road; cul de sac. Brits also share all of the usual meanings of the word.

coach *n* bus. Generally used in the U.K. for longer-haul buses (50 miles or more). The difference between a *coach* and a "bus" is that a coach tends to have a loo, not so much chewing gum attached to the seats and fewer old ladies hacking up phlegm in the back. Brits do not use coach to refer to economy-class seats on an aircraft; that's a peculiar American thing.

cobblers *n* rubbish; nonsense. An informal term; you'd be more likely to use it in response to your mate's claim that he can down fifteen pints in a sitting than while giving evidence in a murder trial. Possibly Cockney rhyming slang, from "cobbler's awls" / "balls." This may be true. Who knows?

Cockney *n* person from the East End of London. Strictly speaking, someone "born within the sound of the bells of Bow Church." A more modern definition might be "born within the sound of a racist beating," "born in the back of a stolen Mercedes" or perhaps "born within the range of a Glock semi-automatic." Cockneys have a distinctive accent, which other Brits are all convinced that they can mimic after a few pints.

cock-up *v* make a complete mess of something: *I went to a job interview today and cocked it up completely.* Brits also use the phrase "balls-up" to mean the same thing. Ironically enough, however, "balls-up" is seen as a lot less rude.

codswallop *n* nonsense. The etymology of this antiquated but superb word leads us to an English gentleman named Hiram Codd, who in 1872 came up with the idea of putting a marble and a small rubber ring just inside the necks of beer bottles in order to keep fizzy beer fizzy ("wallop" being Old English for beer). The idea was that the pressure of the fizz would push the marble against the ring, thereby sealing the bottle. Unfortunately, the thing wasn't nearly as natty as he'd hoped and "Codd's wallop" slid into the language first as a disparaging comment about flat beer and eventually as a general term of abuse.

colleague *n* co-worker. In here because Brits do not use the term "co-worker." Of no relevance at all is the fact that Brits also do not refer to the hosts of television news programmes as "anchors," which caused my British boss some confusion when he became convinced that the CNN presenter had handed over to her "co-wanker."

college *n* an educational establishment which specialises in single-year studies between school and university.

collywobbles *n* spine-tingling fear; heebie jeebies. Originally meant the act or fear of having an unexpected and uncontrolled bowel movement. Which does make one wonder whether "colly" is an accepted abbreviation for "colon." Probably isn't. I'm done with the wondering now.

concessions *n* discounts you might get on things if you've been there before, are a student, are over sixty or such like. Brits do not use the U.S. definition (snacks you buy during a film or sporting event). Often abbreviated "concs," to confuse American tourists attending crappy mainstream musicals in the West End.

cooker *n* machine that does the actual cooking of your food. While this is a peculiarly British term, "oven" is used both in the U.K. and the U.S. to mean exactly the same thing.

cop off *v* snog; French kiss: *I could swear I saw Ian's dad copping off with some woman at the cinema the other day.* The phrase may be derived from a contraction of "copulate." Of course, it doesn't mean "copulate," so perhaps not.

copper *n* policeman. May come from the copper buttons policemen originally wore on their uniforms; may also be derived from the Latin "capere," which means "to capture." In turn, the American word "cop" may be derived from *copper*, although may equally easily be an abbreviation for "Constable on Patrol" or "Constable of the Police." There. I don't think I committed to anything.

cor *interj* ooh! Once a part of the phrase "cor blimey," this is now used on its own to mean something like "ooh!" And here was you thinking that was some sort of typo.

cor blimey *interj* rather older-fashioned term of surprise: *Cor blimey, I thought he was going to drive straight into us!* Has mostly migrated these days into just "blimey" or, more rarely, "cor."

coriander *n* cilantro. The herb that tastes like soap, and redefines the term "edible." Americans still call the fruit of the plant "coriander" but not the leaves.

cot *n* crib. Americans call a sort of frame camp bed a "cot." Brits don't. I'd say they just called it a "camp bed," as God intended. I'm guessing that he intended that. The Bible is fairly ambiguous about which day God chose to create camp beds.

cotton buds *n* cotton swabs, or "Q-Tips." When I came back from Tenerife with an ear infection I deduced had come from swimming in the sea, I got a telling-off from the doctor for attempting to cure myself with the aid of some cotton buds. According to the doctor, you should "never put anything at all into your ear smaller than your elbow." Medical advice dispensed here at no extra cost.

cotton wool *n* cotton ball — the little furry blob that women use to remove makeup and men use to clean inlet manifolds.

council house *n* public housing, projects. Housing built by the government and meted out to the needy, so they can reproduce and smoke pot in it. In the U.K. such projects were largely the brainchild of a Labour government, but when the Conservatives took power in 1979 they had the fantastic idea of allowing the tenants (generally working-class Labour voters) the option of buying their council houses at a discount to market value, which proved wonderfully popular. It also made it rather tricky for Labour to reverse the plan when they attained power in 1997, as it had made a great many of their upstanding supporters substantially richer.

courgette *n* zucchini. I wonder if there's anything behind the fact that these words both look like they ought to be sports cars. I'm sure someone's written a thesis on it somewhere.

court shoes *n* pumps. Lightweight heeled women's dress shoes with enclosed toes.

cowboy *n* dishonest and incompetent tradesman: *I'm not surprised it exploded, it was installed by a bunch of cowboys!*

craic *n pron. "crack"* fun and frolics to be had with other people; what makes a particular pub fun, or a particular wedding bearable: *The pub ended up being a bit shit but the craic was great!* From Irish Gaelic, hence the comedy spelling. The popular recreational drug "crack" exists in the U.K., as does the euphemism for vagina. This means endless confusion for many Irish crack whores.

creche *n* day-care. The place you take your children to be looked after, usually while you bumble off and make the money you'll need to pay for it. The Brits do not use the word to describe a the revolting

Christian Christmas scene that your child brought home from school and you're not sure where to jettison (see "nativity").

crikey *interj* general expression of surprise. Rather elderly and a little esoteric these days — you can most imagine it being used in a context something like: *Crikey, Eustace — looks like Cambridge are going to win after all!* It may be derived from "Christ kill me." It also may not.

crisps *n* potato chips, or any of the corn-based equivalents. It's worth bearing in mind that crisps in the U.K. cover a wide variety of flavours from Worcester Sauce to steak, and are not restricted to tasting anything like a potato. In fact, producing something that tastes anything like a potato is probably a sacking offence in the crisp factory. This particular confusion has caused me no end of troubles in the U.S. — I've never been so disappointed with a "bag of chips" in my life.

cropper *n* sudden failure. Only really used in the phrase "come a cropper," e.g., *Your uncle Arthur came a cropper on his motorcycle one evening after a few beers!* It means something particularly bad has happened to the person in question. Most likely they died.

crumbs *interj* general expression of surprise. Much akin to "God," or "bloody hell" in that context (but without the ghastly use of our saviour's name in vain or any swearing). It's quite all right to use in polite company, though perhaps a little antiquated. More likely to be heard in a context like: *Crumbs, that's more expensive than Harrods* rather than: *Crumbs, I just dropped the smack out the window.*

crumpet *n* **1** small teacake made of pancake batter, but with raising agents added to make holes. **2** loose woman. Coming from rhyming slang for "strumpet" (a woman adulterer), *crumpet* refers to women in a similar (although a little more old-fashioned) way to "totty." Suffice to say that if you were out looking for some *crumpet* of an evening, you wouldn't be intending sleeping alone. In fact, you may not be intending to sleep at all. Despite it meaning, primarily, a small teacake, it would be difficult to mention such a teacake in the U.K. without someone at the table collapsing in fits of giggles.

cuppa *n* cup of tea: *Surely you have time for a cuppa?*

current account *n* checking account. The bank account into which you deposit your salary, only to have it seep away gently through the porous floor of the bank.

curtains *n* any cloth covering a window. Brits don't call the longer ones "drapes."

custard *n* sort of yellow-looking dessert sauce made from egg yolks and milk. It does sound a little disgusting, but you'll have to believe me that it's not. Brits pour it on top of things like apple crumble and sponges (see "sponge").

cutlery *n* silverware. Knives and forks and stuff. Brits therefore do not have the curious American concept of "plastic silverware."

CV *n* résumé. *C.V.* stands for the Latin curriculum vitae, "life's work." Brits don't use "résumé" at all. In North America the term "C.V." is sometimes used to refer to a fairly regimented timeline of academic achievement.

D

daddy long-legs *n* crane fly. Not to be confused with the American "daddy long-legs," which refers to a whole order, Opiliones, also called harvestmen on both sides of the Atlantic.

dado *n* decorative wooden track that some people think is nice to have around walls at the height of a chair back. Those people are blithering morons. Brits also know such a thing as a "dado rail;" Americans call it "molding" or "chair rail." To confuse things slightly, a *dado* to an American carpenter is a slot in a piece of wood (usually for fitting shelves or cabinets) which Brits call a "rebate" or "housing."

daft *adj* not in possession of, well, "the full shilling." Daft can range from the absent-minded: *You've forgotten to put petrol in it, daft woman!* to the criminally insane: *Well, once we let him out of the car boot he went completely daft!*

dago *n* Spanish person (rather uncharitable and slightly antiquated). I mean the term is uncharitable and antiquated, not the Spanish person in question. There are two possible etymologies: One is that it is a slightly abbreviated "Diego," that being of course a popular Spanish name. It may also be a contraction of the town name San Diego (named after Santiago, a.k.a. St. James, the patron saint of Spain). The term is in use in the U.S. but, rather perversely, refers to Italians.

damp *n (yes, noun)* wet rot. You might hear it in a phrase such as: *Bob's moved out of his house as it's been practically destroyed by damp.*

damper *n* shock absorber. The part of a vehicle's suspension system that stops the suspension from bouncing (rather than actually absorbing any shock).

dapper *adj* as befitting someone who is very much the country squire — well-spoken, well-dressed and rather upper-class. Despite once having been a compliment, the recent unpopularity of the upper classes in the U.K. has made this a mild insult.

daylight robbery *n* highway robbery. A swindle so blatant that its very audacity takes you by surprise: *Twenty percent a year? That's bloody daylight robbery!*

dead arm *n* an arm which has been disabled via a punch to the tricep. A popular form of entertainment amongst school bullies or inebriated university students.

dear *adj* expensive. While a little bit antiquated, it's still in pretty widespread use.

demister *n* defroster. The little network of electrical wires that weave around your car's rear window and are intended to remove frost. They are perhaps referred to as such in the U.K. because any devices attached to British-built cars have precious little chance of getting rid of frost, and, indeed, don't stand much of a chance against mist, either.

deplane *v* disembark from an aeroplane. A very antiquated term, it'd be met with a vacant stare by most Brits under forty, as would its antonym, "enplane."

diddle *v* swindle mildly. A colleague might diddle you out of getting the best seats at the game; you'd be less likely to tell of when your grandparents were diddled out of their fortune, leaving them penniless beggars working the streets for cash. Brits do not use the term to refer to onanism.

digestive *n* round biscuit that one generally dunks in one's tea. Whether it aids the digestion or not, who can tell?

dinner *n* *Northern English* mid-day meal. This is a bit of a generalisation — the words *dinner*, "tea," "lunch" and "supper" seem to be assigned to meals spattered randomly around the day in both American and English regional dialects.

divvy 1 *n* idiot. Likely derived from "divot," meaning "clod." Calling someone a *divvy* is pretty tame,

much on a par with telling them they are a "dimwit." **2** divide up (universal).

do *n* party – you might have a drinks *do* to celebrate a new job: *Pat and Jim are having a do to celebrate their fiftieth anniversary.* **stag do** Bachelor Party.

doddle *n* something very easy.

dodgem *n* bumper-car. Once used in U.S. English too, but now chiefly British. Odd that it should imply an aim to the game that is quite the opposite of what it is.

dodgy *adj* something either shady: *I bought it off some dodgy punter in the pub*, sexually suggestive: *The old bloke in the office keeps saying dodgy things to me at the coffee machine*, or simply not quite as things should be: *I got rid of that car; the suspension felt dodgy.* What appalling sentence structure. Fuck it.

dog-end *n* stubbed-out end of a cigarette. More commonly Brits use the international term "butt."

dog's bollocks *n* See "bollocks." I'm not writing it twice.

dog's breakfast *n* something which has been made a complete mess of: *When we finally got his tax return through it turned out it was a dog's breakfast.* Why the dog should have any worse breakfast than the rest of us, I have no idea.

dog's dinner *n* same as "dog's breakfast" (marginally more common).

dogsbody *n* lowly servant. Your *dogsbody* would be the person who polished your shoes, emptied your bins and cleaned your loo. That is, if you were lucky enough to have someone like that.

dole *n* welfare. An allocation of money that the government gives to unemployed people, ostensibly to help them eat and clothe themselves during their fervent search for gainful employment but really for buying fags and lager. **on the dole** receiving welfare: *Bob's been on the dole since his accident.*

donkey's years *n* ages; a very long time: *That shop's been there for donkey's years.* The term originates from the fact that donkeys are larger than human beings, and so if we were all planets then years would be longer on the donkey-planet than they would on the human-planet. This is certainly the most likely explanation.

dosh *n* money. A fairly London-based term until being popularised by the Harry Enfield pop song "Loadsamoney."

doss *v* sit about not doing much. You might describe one of your less-productive colleagues as a *dosser*, because he (or she, I suppose — laziness is not quite confined to males) sits around *dossing* all the time instead of working.

double-barrelled *adj* surname which consists of two hyphenated names, such as "Rhys-Jones" or "Fox-Kelton."

dozy *adj* perhaps most kindly characterised as "slow." Someone described as *dozy* might be a little sluggish in understanding things.

draught *n pron. "draft"* the flap inside the chimney of an open fire which you can open or close to allow more or less air into the hearth. Americans know it better as a "damper," which is a part of car suspension in the U.K.

draughts *n pron. "drafts"* two-player board game where each player gets sixteen pieces and takes the opponent's by jumping over them diagonally. I mean the pieces jump diagonally, not the players. Though it's an interesting point as to whether two people could really jump over one another diagonally, given that the vector is relative to the positions of them both. In the U.S. the game is known as "checkers."

drawing-pin *n* thumb-tack. A pin with a fairly large flat head. So called because they were once used to draw blood during satanic rituals. I just guessed that one, it might be wrong.

dressing gown *n* bathrobe; the outfit that you wear if you're an attractive young lady coming out of the bath to answer the door in a coffee advertisement. Or if you're Hugh Heffner. Ah, the great contradictions of modern life.

dual carriageway *n* divided highway. There is generally very little difference between a dual carriageway and a motorway except that learner drivers are not allowed onto motorways.

dummy 1 *n* pacifier. One of those teat-things you put in babies' mouths to stop them crying. **2** idiot (universal); mannequin (universal).

Durex *n* condom. In the U.K., Durex is a large (possibly the largest, I'm not sure) manufacturer of condoms, and the brand name once slipped into the language (no pun intended). The term is actually becoming less common these days. A very similar thing happened in the U.S. with "Trojan." As an aside, *Durex*, to an Australian, is sticky-tape (a.k.a. Scotch tape). I don't know if they use it as a contraceptive, and I don't wish to think about it any further.

dustbin *n* trashcan. Can't think of anything particularly witty to add.

dustman *n* garbage man, trash collector. I presume "dustwoman" is also appropriate in these heady days of sexual equality.

duvet *n* comforter. In the U.K. one sleeps on top of a sheet and directly under the duvet – Brits do not layer sheets underneath it.

Dux *n* "best student" of a class year. Fairly old-fashioned, this is now only used in private schools. I'm told that Americans have "valedictorians" instead, which somehow sounds much grander.

dynamo *n* generator. Usually on a car or bicycle, this is a device intended to take power from the engine to recharge your battery as you drive along (or power the lights, in the case of a bicycle). Or, in the case of my own fine automobile, take power from the engine and dribble it lazily into the ether. These days, *dynamos* on cars have been replaced by alternators. Alternators run on alternating current as opposed to direct current and are more effective at charging the battery at low revs. Why, you might wonder, do some of the parts

of this book that relate to cars appear to have a lot more effort put into them than other parts? Well, I'm a car person. I'm much more interested in car words than I am in words that mean "sheetrock" or "faucet." If you're a sheetrock person then I'm sure there's a book out there somewhere for you.

E

Ecosse *n* what the French call Scotland. It's in here only because *The Sunday Times* newspaper uses the word as a section title. The word is also known reasonably widely around the U.K. — the only Scottish motor-racing team anyone's ever heard of was called "Ecurie Ecosse." Also means some other thing in French but I have no idea what.

eejit *n* idiot. I can only guess that it is derived from something like a phonetic representation of an Irish person saying exactly that.

Elastoplast *n* adhesive bandage, i.e. Band-Aid. Antiquated term – "Plaster" is used more commonly in modern British English.

elevenses *n* mid-morning snack. Rather old-fashioned; clearly derived somehow from eleven o'clock.

engaged *adj* busy, as in a telephone line. Many sit-coms have sustained plot lines built around the truly hilarious "engaged in a phone call/engaged to be married" mix-up.

enplane *v* get onto an aeroplane. As out of use as its sister word, "deplane."

entrée *n* appetizer. Only in America does this not mean "appetizer." Why, in America, a word that clearly means "enter" or "start" means "main course" is beyond me. Perhaps it's because American appetizers are about the size of everyone else's main courses.

estate agent *n* real estate agent, realtor — the person who carefully listens to all your whims and fancies about the sort of home you'd like, and then takes you to see one that doesn't fulfil any of those criteria but they're having trouble selling.

estate car *n* station wagon.

F

faff *v* pussyfoot; bumble about doing things that aren't quite relevant to the task in hand. You'll often find it used when men are complaining about women faffing around trying on different sets of clothes before going out, which uses up valuable drinking time.

fag 1 *n* cigarette. In very widespread use. One of the most amusing emails I've had concerning this word was from an American who had arrived at her company's U.K. offices to be told that the person she was looking for was "outside blowing a fag." **2** *n* first year senior-school kids who have to perform menial tasks (cleaning boots, running errands and the like) for the seniors (slightly antiquated). Another email tells me of a man who was met with aghast looks when he told a group of New Yorkers that he "was a fag at school last year." Modern thinking on slavery has seen that the practice of *fagging* all but die out.

faggot 1 *n* particular variety of sausage. **2** *n* bundle of sticks. **3** *n* grumpy old woman (uncommon). **4** *n* cigarette (uncommon). **5** *n* prostitute (uncommon). Brits do not use it as a derisive term for a homosexual man. In reality, the American definition is well known (if not really used) U.K.-wide, so most of the jokes involving the various other meanings have already been made. They all stem from the original Norse word "fagg," meaning a bundled-together collection of matter. Do prostitutes come in bundles, I wonder.

fairy lights *n* Christmas lights. I'd like to describe these by reading from an entry in a fictional encyclopaedia for aliens: Human beings celebrate Christmas by cutting the top off a tree, moving it to a pot in their living room, covering it with small electrical lights and standing a small model of a woman on its tip. As it dies, they drink alcohol, sing to it and give it gifts.

fancy *v* be attracted to; have a crush on. Seen in contexts like, *I really fancy that chap from the coffee shop* or: *Hey, Stu, I think that bird over there fancies you!* Also has several other meanings which are universal.

fancy dress *n* costume (as in costume party). To an American, *fancy dress* means a jacket and tie. To a Brit, *fancy dress* means a cravat, a strap-on wooden leg and a plastic parrot.

fanny *n* female genitalia. This is another word which could leave you abroad and in dire straits. In the U.S., your *fanny* is your posterior and a "fanny pack" is what Brits decided to call a "bum bag" instead. There's a neoprene belt sold in the U.S. that is designed to stop snow from entering your ski jacket during a fall. It is marketed under the name "Fanny Flaps." It is not for sale in the U.K.

film *n* movie. Brits don't go to the theatre to see movies; they go to the cinema to see *films*. They do understand the American word, they just don't use it.

filth *n* police force. Slightly-less-than-complimentary. I ought to mention at this juncture that just because words are in this fine tome doesn't mean to say that I use them regularly.

fit *adj* attractive, when used to describe members of the opposite sex. Very similar to "tidy." A "fit bird" is a fine specimen of the fairer sex, and one described as "fit as a butcher's dog" might be particularly nice.

fizzy drink *n* carbonated drinks. A generic term much like "soda" or perhaps "pop."

flag *adj* become tired; wane: *I was doing fine until the last lap and then I started to flag.*

flannel 1 *n* slightly old-fashioned homonym for "face-cloth," which is in turn a British term which means "washcloth." Hope that's cleared that one up. **2** *n* nonsense; drivel: *I watched the Prime Minister's statement on telly this morning but it was just a bunch of flannel.*

flat *n* apartment or condominium. Derived from the Germanic Old English word "flet," meaning "floor" (a flat occupies only one floor of a building).

flatmate *n* roommates.

floater *n* number-two which refuses to be flushed away. It is not, as one of my contributors discovered, an appropriate name for laptop that's shared around various parts of the office.

flog 1 *n* sell. Has an air of poor credibility to it — a bloke in the pub might *flog* you a dodgy car stereo, but you're less likely to find Marks and Spencer announcing in the press that from next week they'll be flogging a new ladies wear range. Americans would probably use "hawk" in the same instances. **2** beat viciously (universal).

fluff *n* lint. More than simply lint, *fluff* stretches to cover any unexpected bits of hair/fur/fabric, appearing anywhere from the corner of your living room to your posterior.

flutter *v* brief, low-stake foray into gambling. Many people "have a flutter" on the Grand National horse race once a year, or the odd boxing match. Anything more regular and it's just straight gambling.

fly tipping *v* unauthorised waste disposal – most often seen in signs declaring "no fly tipping" which have been hastily erected next to popular sites for dumping stuff. Originates from a time when houseflies were employed to remove garbage from the house, which they did using tiny little bags strapped to their legs. They would then fly in convoy to the *fly tipping* site and simultaneously unload their cargo, the whole event looking like a strange miniature reconstruction of the firebombing of Dresden. This, obviously, is a wholly incorrect etymology, but I can't be bothered checking it. "But," I hear you say, "The internet is just over there. Why don't you just look?" Well, my web browser is closed. And my boss is coming.

football *n* soccer. Americans call a different game "football." It doesn't require much involvement from feet, and they don't have a proper ball. Brits call that "American football." I have a theory about the relative popularities of soccer in the U.K. and American football in the U.S., upon which I shall now expound. In life in general, British people tend to put up with the status quo and keep their fingers crossed, rather than make any conscious effort towards striving for success. Until success lands miraculously upon their doorstep, Brits will pass the time moaning about how difficult their lives are. Americans, on the other hand, like to feel that they're entirely in control of their own destiny and can shape it in any way they see fit. Americans will go out actively seeking success, and until it arrives they will mercilessly

criticise themselves for not trying hard enough to find it. Bear with me, the point is approaching. Soccer is a game with very low scores – it's not uncommon for a game to end with no scoring at all by either team. American football, on the other hand, has scoring aplenty. The net result of this is that a fairly poor soccer team can win a game just by being a bit lucky. This proves to Brits that success truly is a random thing, and they just need to keep waiting. A bad American football team will never win a game. This proves to Americans that hard work pays off, and that they should continue to better themselves in whatever way they can.

footpath *n* any path usable on foot — it can refer to ones used for hiking or just the sidewalk.

fortnight *n* two weeks. This word is in very common usage in the U.K. As to why the Brits need a term for a time period which the Americans have never felt the urge to name, perhaps it stems from the fact that Americans get so little annual leave that they can never really take a *fortnight* of holiday anyway.

fringe 1 *n* bangs. The bits of hair coming down over your forehead. So called because it's the fringe of your hair. Americans call them "bangs" because they look like small explosions of hair emitting from the scalp. **2** the edge of something (universal).

fry-up *n* meal (almost always breakfast) consisting of mostly fried stuff (sausage, eggs, bacon and the like). Ideal for those seeking heart disease.

full Monty, the *n* the works; the whole shebang. Since the 1997 film of the same name the phrase has tended to mean "completely naked" if not put in a context.

full stop *n* period. The little dot at the end of a sentence, not the part of the menstrual cycle. Brits also use *full stop* for emphasis the same way that Americans use "period": *And I says to him, I'm not putting up with this any more, full stop.*

G

gaffe *n* home. Rather a London-centric word: *Why don't we go back to my gaffe and skin up?* The shorter word "gaff" (to make a foolish error) is the same in both U.K. and U.S. English.

gaffer *n* bloke in charge. Originally the foreman of a construction site, but can be used universally. In the film industry, the *gaffer* is the set's chief electrician, in charge of pretty much anything with wires attached to it. This may or may not be relevant.

gaffer tape *n* duct tape. Sort of. The heavy, slightly meshed sticky tape used to silence potential murder victims and to reliably and effectively attach small animals to tables. Unlike duct tape, *gaffer tape* is designed not to melt onto things, and is used extensively in the theatre and film industry. Probably derived from the fact that the Gaffer is the chief electrician on a film set.

garden *n* back yard. Americans use the word "garden" to refer to areas where fairly specific things are grown – flowers or vegetables, for example. Brits use the word to refer to the area behind their house which contains some grass, a long-since abandoned attempt at a rockery and a broken plastic tricycle.

gazump *n* accept a higher offer in a property deal at the very last minute: *The day we were supposed to sign the papers we were gazumped! Your mother spat at them, which made me feel slightly better about it.*

G-clamp *n* C-clamp. I'd say they look more like 'G's. If you've no idea what any of this means, don't worry your pretty little head about it.

gear lever *n* the "stick" of a stick-shift car. This applies to cars with manual transmission - automatic cars in the U.K. are reserved for pensioners, the severely disabled and Americans.

gearbox *n* transmission. The box of gears that sits between the engine and the prop shaft of a car.

geezer *n* dude. While Americans use *geezer* too, it implies someone much older and with much less street-cred than the British version: *Is that yours? / Sort of, I just bought it off some geezer in the pub. / Was it always that colour? / I think it might be dead.*

Geordie *n* person from Newcastle, or thereabouts.

get off *v* make out: *I just noticed Ian's ex getting off with his* *brother!* This must not be confused with the U.S. term "to get someone off," which means, well, rather a lot more.

get your end away *v* have sex: *I think our dog's been getting his end away with that St. Bernard down the street.*

giddy *n* dizzy or vertiginous. In the U.S. this means silliness and/or giggling - the British definition is more of a medical condition. The British driving license application form asks the applicant whether they are "subject to excessive giddiness."

git *n* a tricky one to define. But, of course, that's what I'm getting paid the big bucks for. What it doesn't mean is what The Waltons meant when they said it ("git outta here, John-Boy"). *Git* is technically an insult but has a twinge of jealousy to it. You'd call someone a *git* if they'd won the Readers' Digest Prize Draw, outsmarted you in a battle of wits or been named in Bill Gates' last will and testament because of a spelling mistake. Like "sod," it has a friendly tone to it. It may be derived from Arabic, or it may be a contraction of the word "illegitimate." Or neither.

give over *interj* give up: *When are you going to stop watching telly and get your homework done? / Jesus mum, give over!*

give way *interj* yield. This phrase on a road sign means that, at the junction you're approaching, other traffic has the right of way. The signs themselves are white upward-pointing triangles with a red line

around them; Americans have downward-pointing yellow ones with "Yield" written on them.

glass *v* the act of breaking a glass and shoving the lower half of it into someone's face, thereby causing some degree of distress. A popular way for pikeys to settle arguments.

gob 1 *n* mouth. Almost always used in the context "shut your gob." **2** *v* spit: *The pikey fucker just gobbed down my shirt!* It's possible the word is derived from Gaelic, where it means a bird's beak, or from the English navy, where it was used widely to refer to the toilet.

gobshite *n* *Scottish* **1** bullshit. Intended to refer to the metaphorical shite that is coming out of your gob: *Jimmy said he was in the Olympic ski team but to be honest I think it's all gobshite.* **2** the person who is emitting said matter: *I wouldn't believe anything Anne says, she's a wee gobshite.*

gobsmacked *adj* surprised; taken aback: *I was completely gobsmacked... I didn't even know she was pregnant.*

golf buggy *n* golf cart. The device intended to remove the only useful part of golf (some exercise) from the sport.

googly *n* a cricket ball bowled such that it bounces unpredictably when it lands.

Gordon Bennett *interj* Christ. By this I don't mean that Britain is under the grip of a strange new religion where Jesus Christ has been replaced by a man called Gordon Bennett, who came to earth in the guise of a used car salesman to save humanity from eternal damnation. No, I mean more that this is a general-purpose expletive, used in a similar context to "Christ!" or "Bollocks!": *Your brother Tommy's won the lottery! / Gordon Bennett!* Its source lies in the mid-19th century with James Gordon Bennett, son of the founder of the New York Herald and Associated Press (who was also called Gordon Bennett, in case you thought this was going to be simple). Born with cash to spare, Gordon Jr. became legendary for high-roller stunts and fits of notoriety including urinating in his in-laws' fireplace, and burning money in public. His name entered the lexicon as a term of exclamation for anything a bit over the top.

gormless *adj* slightly lacking in the common sense department; a bit daft. The word (as "gaumless") also exists in Scots-derived American English with the same meaning but is not in common use.

grammar *n* textbook. A very antiquated term – would be met with blank stares by most schoolchildren these days. Can't think of anything witty to add. If you're sitting there working on a "grammar / grandma" joke, please don't. Whatever it was, my father has probably already used it.

grass 1 *n* snitch; informer. **2** *v* inform. Normally used in the context of criminals *grassing on* each other to the police, but I certainly remember being *grassed up* at school for going to McDonalds instead of Modern Studies. If I could remember who it was who squealed, I'd name and shame him but right at this very minute I can't recall. **3** marijuana (universal).

green fingers *n* green thumbs. A characteristic of a person particularly good at looking after plants. Difficult to imagine how these two different terms arose, but there you go.

grope *n* fondle (in a sexual fashion): *As soon as the lights went out, Bob groped her and she kicked him in the nuts. I knew he'd do something like that eventually but I don't think any of us expected him to do it at a funeral.*

grizzle *n Scottish* grumble or moan. Much like "whinging." Often used to refer to grumpy babies: *Oh, just ignore him he's been grizzling all morning.*

grotty *adj* gross; disgusting. Your mother might use it to describe your room, or your girlfriend might use it to describe your whole flat. Or maybe you're cleaner than I am.

guff 1 *v* fart. Presumably some sort of derivation of "chuff" or vice versa. Not to be confused with "gaff." **2** *n* verbiage: *I asked him what happened, but he just gave me a load of guff.*

Guinea *n* old unit of currency in the U.K. Worth "one pound and one shilling," a Guinea coin was minted from 1731 until 1813. The somewhat curious value is due to the fact that it was created largely to cater for auction-houses, where for each pound the seller receives for his goods, the auctioneer takes a shilling (5%). The buyer, therefore, pays a Guinea.

gutted *adj* deeply disappointed. You might use it to describe your state of health after your football team were beaten eight-nil and you dropped your car keys in a pond.

guv'nor *n London* the boss. While I've no doubt this derives from the word "governor," I can guarantee that you'll never hear the missing letters being pronounced or even written.

gyp *n* irritating pain: *I don't think I'll make it out tonight; my ankle is giving me gyp.* Interestingly, in the U.S. "gypping" is cheating.

H

haggis *n* small Scottish mammal, known better for the unpleasant-tasting dish it is often made into. There has been a lot of concern in Scotland lately that over-farming may endanger the remaining population - if you want to help, please voice your concerns to The World-Wide Fund for Nature. Make it clear that you're an American, and that you were made aware of the poor creature's plight by this fine piece of work.

haha *n* trench dug at the edge of one's garden as a replacement for a fence, so that the view from the garden to the surrounding countryside is unspoiled, but you aren't going to be deluged by animals or grotty peasants from the village. There seems to be some validity to the idea that they are so-called because of the surprise at coming across one whilst out walking.

handbrake *n* emergency brake (on a car). A *handbrake* operates like a normal brake pedal but only on the rear wheels. Before the days of speed-cameras, Brits used to use the *handbrake* to slow down when they passed police cars as the brake lights don't go on and it's not so obvious you were speeding.

hand-luggage *n* carry-on baggage. Belongings you are intending carrying into an aeroplane rather than checking into the hold.

hard *adj* tough. A "hard man" is a tough guy, someone who won't take any flack. This amuses Americans, for obvious reasons.

hard shoulder *n* shoulder. The poorly-surfaced bit at the side of the road that you're only supposed to drive on if you've broken down, have fallen asleep at the wheel or desperately need to wee.

hash *n* pound; octathorp (the symbol '#'). As well as various other universal meanings, Brits call the '#' symbol *hash*.

haver *v* *Scottish pron. "hay-ver"* ramble incoherently: *I went to see granny at the weekend but, well, bless her, she's just havering these days.* The word is in common usage, and features in the Proclaimers' song *I'm Gonna Be (500 miles).*

having kittens *interj* extremely nervous: *I was having kittens beforehand but once I got in there the director explained the plot and I managed to just get undressed and get on with it.*

head boy *n* highest-achieving pupil - synonymous with Dux.

hen-night *n* Bachelorette Party. The girls-only night out before a wedding. It seems to be a legal requirement that the bride is wearing a wedding dress, some traffic cones and L-plates and that everybody but the bride ends up sleeping with some random bloke, just to annoy her.

higgledy-piggledy *adj* in disarray; jumbled up. You might use it to describe the garden shed you built when you got home from the pub. The term is a little antiquated but still in use.

high tea *n* a light meal usually consisting of sandwiches, tea and scones and served in the late afternoon. It's now rather restricted to the upper classes (who have nothing better to do in the afternoons) but many posh London hotels serve it, for an appropriately preposterous sum of money.

high-street *n* main street. The main road through somewhere. Nowhere in particular. Could be anywhere. Although, thinking about it, it would probably have to be somewhere in the U.K.

hill-walking *n* hiking. The term "hiking" is also used in the U.K. You didn't really need to look this up in a dictionary, did you. You really couldn't work it out? What is this "hill walking" of which you speak? What could it entail?

hire *v* rent. Americans rent rental-cars; Brits *hire hire-cars*. In the U.K., the word extends to any other objects you might borrow for a short period of time - bicycles, bulldozers, hookers and such like.

Americans will only ever use the word "hire" in connection with hiring a person to perform a task, not a machine.

hob *n* rangetop; stovetop. The top bit of a cooker with the burners on it, where you put pans and things.

hockey *n* field hockey. To a Brit, *hockey* is played on grass. "Ice hockey" is played on ice.

holiday *n* vacation. What an American would call a "holiday," a Brit would call a "public holiday" or a "bank holiday." Scotland and England have bank holidays on different dates, presumably to stop the Scots and English meeting up and fighting in popular seaside towns.

hood *n* convertible top. The part of a convertible car that, well, converts. This only serves to complicate the bonnet/boot confusion. Brits do not use "hood" as an abbreviation of "neighbourhood," unless they are trying to act like American rap stars. Brits are not very good at that, although it doesn't stop them trying.

hoover *n* vacuum cleaner. **–ing** *v* vacuuming. The Hoover Company was an early manufacturer of vacuum cleaners, though originally they were invented by a company called British Vacuumation. Where are they now? They could have cleaned up. Sorry.

how's your father *n* sex. Often used in the phrase "a bit of how's your father" and generally accompanied by a knowing wink. It's rather antiquated, but well understood.

hum *n* unusually bad smell, perhaps somewhat associated with rottenness. Is rottenness a word? Who knows?

I

icing sugar *n* powdered/confectioner's sugar. The very fine sugar used to make cake icing.

ickle *n* itty-bitty; very small. Usually be seen in use regarding "cute" things: *What an ickle puppy!* Less likely to be seen in more serious situations: *Dad - I've just had an ickle accident in your car.*

indeed *adv* extra-much, when used after a statement: *It was pretty warm to start with but when they turned on the booster rockets it got very hot indeed.*

indicator *n* turn signal. The little orange lights that flash on the side of the car to show that you're about to frantically try and turn across four lanes of traffic into your driveway.

innit *interj London* "isn't it." A very London-centric contraction with nasal pronunciation obligatory: *Well, the traffic's always this bad at this time of night, innit guvnor.*

interval *n* intermission. The break in a stage performance where the audience can go off to have a pee and get some more beers in. At a stretch it could refer to the period of time in which advertisements are shown on television, though Brits more commonly refer to that as the "break."

ironmonger *n* hardware shop. A bit of an antiquated word.

jabs *n* inoculations: *I'm off to the Amazon for a week – got to get my jabs this morning!*

jacket potato *n* baked potato. A potato baked in its skin and usually filled with something. The term "baked potato" is equally well understood in the U.K.

jam *n* jelly. Sort of. What Americans call "jelly" (fruit preserve without fruity-bits in it), Brits still call *jam*. What Americans call "jello," Brits call "jelly." Oh yes, and what Americans call "jam" is still also called *jam* in the U.K. I think that's the jams pretty much covered.

jammy *adj* lucky. Often seen in the phrase "you jammy git," uttered graciously on some sort of defeat.

jam-sandwich *n* police car. Also "jam butty." So called because they are white, with a red stripe down the middle, and therefore are almost indistinguishable from a twelve-foot metal jam sandwich.

jelly *n* Jell-o. Gelatinous sweet desert. The Jell-o brand doesn't exist in the U.K.

jiffy *n* moment; very short period of time: *I'll be there in a jiffy!* The phrase comes from a time before Jiffy was a popular brand of condom.

John Thomas *n* penis. The term derives from the name given to the appendage of the leading man in D.H. Lawrence's novel, *Lady Chatterley's Lover*. The book was made famous by the obscenity trial it landed Penguin Books in during the 1950s. Someone once told me that in America one could buy "John Thomas relish" to put on your lunch. This turned out to be nonsense, but is somehow still amusing. Perhaps I'll invent it.

joint *n* large side of meat, like a Sunday roast. The Brits, like the Americans, also use the word to refer to cannabis spliffs, which means that these days you'd be unlikely to get away with referring to your "Sunday joint" without someone giggling.

jolly *adv* **1** very: *We had a jolly good time at the zoo.* **2** *adj* happy: *He seemed remarkably jolly about the whole business.*

jumble sale *n* garage sale; yard sale. The wonderful event where people get together in order to sell the revolting tacky rubbish they've accumulated over the years.

jump leads *n* jumper cables. The pair of heavy wires which you use to connect the battery of your working car to the battery of your dead car, or to a person from whom you wish to extract information.

jumper *n* sweater. What Americans call a "jumper" (a set of overalls

with a skirt instead of trousers),
Brits would call a "pinafore."

K

kagoul *n* wind breaker; poncho. A light waterproof jacket, usually one that zips up into an unfeasibly small self-contained package. The word derives from the French "cagoule" (meaning much the same thing), which in turn comes from the Latin "cuculla," meaning "hood." In the U.S. technical theatre industry a "kagoul" is a black hood worn by magicians' stagehands to render them invisible-ish. I once thought about writing a whole book dedicated to the word "kagoul," but then decided against it.

kecks *n* pants (U.S. pants); trousers. May come from India, where "kachs" are loose-fitting trousers with a low crotch.

kerb *n* curb. Not entirely sure how the different spellings arose.

kerfuffle *n Scottish* big fuss; rumpus. The word "fuffle" (meaning to dishevel) arrived in Scottish English in the 16th century; the word gained a "car-" in the 19th, to arrive in the 20th with its current spelling.

khasi *n pron. "kah-zee"* toilet: *I'm away to the khasi to drain the lizard.* Less likely in more refined conversation: *Excuse me, madam - could you direct me to the khasi?* It may be derived from Arabic. This might not be true. People lie to me all the time.

kip *n* sleep: *I'm just off home for an hour for some kip.* It's a Dutch word meaning a rather run-down place to sleep.

Kirby grip *n* Bobby pin. The little pins you poke in your hair to keep it in place.

kit *n* sports uniform (e.g. rugby kit, football kit). More generally in the U.K., *kit* refers to the equipment necessary to perform a particular task - usually, though not always, sporting. The boundary is woolly to such a degree that it's difficult to generalise - I've heard all sorts of things from parachutes to computers referred to as "kit." **nice piece of kit** an item particularly good at performing its task in hand. Again it could refer to pretty much anything, though I think you'd be more likely to describe your new camera as a *nice piece of kit* than, say, your fiancé.

kitchen roll *n* paper towel. The disposable paper cloth, much akin to a larger, stronger version of toilet paper, that one generally keeps in the kitchen and uses to mop up bits of food and drink that have been inadvertently thrown around. So called, I'd imagine, because Brits keep it in the kitchen and it comes on a roll. Americans call it "paper towel," no doubt because it's made of paper and works like a towel.

Kiwi *n* New Zealander: *We tried this other bar but it was full of drunk Kiwis.* Also an abbreviated name for a Kiwi fruit.

knackered *adj* very tired; beat. Has a slightly more dodgy meaning as it technically describes being exhausted after sex. You can get away with it in everyday conversation but bear in mind that everyone knows the true meaning too. The "knacker's yard" was once a place where old horses were converted into glue. Where the sexual connotations came from is anyone's guess.

knees-up *n* party. A rather antiquated word. A knees-up is more likely to involve some post-menopausal ladies singing around a piano than a bunch of bright young things doing lines off the coffee table.

knickers *n* women's underpants. In old-fashioned English and American English, "knickers" (an abbreviation of the Dutch-derived word "knickerbockers") are knee-length trousers most often seen nowadays on golfers.

knob *also occasionally "nob"* **1** *n* penis. As well as referring to the part of the body, it can be used as an insult. **2** *v* screw; bone. This implies active use of said penis and is similar to "shag." This word appears regularly in American place names, much to the amusement of Brits. Two British

favourites are Bald Knob, Arkansas and Knob Lick, Missouri.

knock about *n* sport practise: *Jimmy and I are taking the football to the park for a knockabout.*

knock up *v* bang upon someone's door, generally to get them out of bed: *OK, g'night - can you knock me up in the morning?* In U.S. English, "knocking someone up" means getting them pregnant. Although most Brits will feign innocence, they do know the U.S. connotations of the phrase and it adds greatly to the enjoyment of using it. Both Brits and Americans share the term "knocking off," to mean various other things.

L

lad *n* **1** young boy. **2** bloke doing blokey things, generally including but not limited to getting pissed (in the U.K. sense); trying to pull birds; making a lot of noise and causing some good wholesome criminal damage. Various derivations have sprung up, with "laddish" covering this type of behaviour and "laddettes" being girls doing much the same thing.

ladder *n* run. In the sense of a "ladder in your tights" being the British equivalent of a "run in your pantyhose." In all other circumstances, this word means exactly the same in the U.K. as it does in the U.S.

ladybird *n* ladybug. Probably nothing to do with Lyndon Johnson's wife, but who can tell.

lairy *adj* noisy, and perhaps a bit abusive: *It was all going fine until Ian's cousin had a couple of drinks too many and started getting lairy.* As usual when it comes to Brits being noisy, it generally involves drinking. They're pretty quiet the rest of the time.

lay-by *n* rest area. A little parking area off the side of a main road (usually a motorway), where people generally stop to have a sandwich, let their children vomit, empty the dog or copulate with their work colleagues. Perhaps this is where the name came from.

Left Luggage *n* a place (usually in a railway station) where you can dump your belongings for a time while you bumble around shopping, or whatever takes your fancy.

leg over *n* sex: *Bob's off to the local again this evening for a few drinks - I think he's still trying to get his leg over with the barmaid who works Thursdays.*

lemonade *n* a clear, carbonated drink very similar to *Sprite* or *7-Up*, but with only lemons instead of limes. In the U.S. (and in the U.K., but under the moniker "traditional lemonade") the word "lemonade" refers to a variant that, for want of a better description, is a bit more lemony. It's darker in colour, not carbonated and often contains bits of lemon. Nowadays young drinkers on street corners in both the U.K. and the U.S. enjoy alcopop lemonade ("hard lemonade"), which is carbonated on both sides of the Atlantic. By that I don't mean it's carbonated on one side of the Atlantic, then flown over and carbonated on the other prior to sale. But you knew that.

lie-in *n* the act of staying in bed longer than you normally would.

Very similar to "sleeping in," though it implies something a little more deliberate. "Sorry, I was having a lie-in" would be as bad an excuse for being late for work as "sorry, I couldn't be arsed getting up."

lift *n* elevator. The word derives from when the devices were once called "lifting rooms."

light *n* car window. Largely obsolete - most seen in modern English inside the term "quarterlights," which is used to refer to those small windows a little ahead of the front door windows, near where the mirrors are attached. "Light" is used in the U.S. architecturally to refer to the individual panes of a split window. The etymology of the term is nautical - small prisms were inserted in the decks of sailing ships to improve visibility below deck, and these themselves became known as "lights."

lodger *n* renter. A person who rents a room in your home. They help pay the bills, provide a little human company on those long, lonely evenings and are a perfect vehicle for your perverted sexual fantasies. A bit like a flatmate but on a less equal footing ownership-wise.

loft *n* attic. The small space in the rafters of your house where you keep letters from your ex-lovers and all of your school books, just in case they might ever come in handy again. The word "attic" is also used in the U.K.

lolly *n* **1** money. **2 ice-** popsicle. A sort of frozen sugary flavoured lump wrapped around a small bit of

wood and designed specifically to drip all down your front as it defrosts.

loo *n* restroom. The derivation comes from a long time ago. As derivations often do, now I think about it. What a lot of nonsense there is in here. Anyway, back then people used to shout "gardez l'eau" (the French equivalent of "look out for the water") and throw their human waste out of the window onto gutters in the street. Of course, it wasn't water at all, but perhaps we were all a bit too posh to shout "gardez le merde." Another almost definitely spurious etymology is that in large mansions the toilet was always numbered room one-hundred to save any embarrassing confusions.

lorry *n* truck. Not a pick-up truck (which barely exist in the U.K.); more of a goods truck.

L-plates *n* big white square stickers with a red letter "L" in them, which have to be put on the front and back of a car that's being driven by a learner driver (i.e. someone on a provisional license). There's no real American equivalent.

lurgy *n* a general diagnosis for any sort of minor sickness which you're not sure of the exact affliction. Could cover anything from the common cold to food poisoning. Or streptococcal meningitis, if you're particularly poor at self-diagnosis. It can also be used as a substitute for the American "cooties."

luv *n* honey; darlin'. A term of endearing address used predominantly by shop staff. You'd hear "that'll be four fifty, luv" in very similar circumstances to those in which you'd hear "that'll be four fifty, honey" in the U.S. It doesn't mean they love you, in either case.

luvvie *n* rather over exuberant (and almost invariably gay) thespian. Referring to actors as "luvvies" or "luvvie darlings" is rather scornful and demeaning - it's true, though, that a few of the older, camper actors do indeed refer to each other as "luvvie."

M

Mac *n* **1** (abbr. of "Macintosh") light waterproof jacket which can usually be squashed up into an impressively small size for packing away. Possibly derived from the name of the gentleman who worked out how to infuse rubber and cloth. Americans call the same sort of thing a "slicker." **2** buddy: *Are you alright Mac?* The two meanings appear together in the *Bonzo Dog Doodah Band*'s song "Big Shot," which features the lines: *On the way home a punk stopped me: "You got a light, mac?" / I said "No, but I've got a dark brown overcoat."*

mad *adj* crazy. Brits do not use the term "mad" to refer to people who are pissed off. Describing something as *mad* (a party, or a weekend away or something) generally means it was riotous fun.

manky *adj* gross; disgusting. The word is derived from the French "manqué," the past participle of "manquer" (to fail).

manual gearbox *n* stick-shift transmission. The way God intended cars to be driven.

Marmite *n* a sandwich spread based upon yeast extract. Similar to "Bovril," which is made from beef extract. Australians have a very similar spread called "Vegemite," which is a little less sharp in taste.

marrow *n* squash. The vegetable.

mate *n* good friend; buddy. It's in very common use in the U.K. and doesn't have any implication that you might want to mate with the person in question. It is derived from "shipmate."

maths *n* mathematics. How the Brits ended up with *maths* and the Americans ended up with "math," I've no idea.

mean *adj* cheap; tight; stingy with money. Brits do not use the word to mean "nasty." So when a Brit talks about his auntie Enid being "mean," he's more likely to mean mean mean what a useful word this is that she's sitting on a million pounds under her mattress rather than she tweaks his ears every time he goes to visit.

mews *n* a short, narrow (often cobbled) street. The word traditionally meant a stable that had been converted into a house, but is now only used to refer to the sort of street they would have been on. Mews houses in central London tend to afford some peace and quiet, and are therefore highly sought after and breathtakingly expensive.

miffed *adj* pissed off: *She was pretty quiet all evening and then got a bit miffed as soon as I suggested we pay half each. She started crying,* *saying she'd never wanted to go to a strip bar in the first place and asking for her purse back.*

milometer *n* odometer. The thing that tells you how far you've gone in the car. A fairly antiquated term.

mince pie *n* a sweet pie, traditionally served at Christmas, containing suet and mixed fruit. Not mincemeat. Step away from the mincemeat. No mincemeat to see here. Traditionally they did contain mincemeat, as the easiest way to preserve meat was to mince it and then mix it with various fruits. Actually, that probably isn't the easiest way at all. The easiest way is probably to bury it in salt. Anyway - the animals having been slaughtered prior to the onset of winter, the mince pies were enjoyed at Christmas because the "preserved" meat was by then pretty much ready to walk out the door by itself. But it was okay, because everyone was kinda drunk.

mince *n* ground beef.

mind *v* watch out for: *Mind the gap*; *Mind your head whilst going down the stairs.*

minge *n* lady's front bottom. The etymology may be Romany.

minger *adj. pron. "ming-er"* someone breathtakingly unattractive: *She looked okay when we were in the bar, but when I woke up the next morning it turned out she was a complete minger.* On fire and put out with a shovel, that sort of thing.

mobile phone *n* cell phone. Can't think of anything witty. Tough shit.

Move onto the next word. Get on with your life.

moggy *n* cat. Implies a cat marginally more streetwise than your average "kitty." A cat which has graduated from the university of life, if you will.

Mole grip *n* **1** one of those fiendishly complicated wrench-type devices which can have its tension adjusted by means of a screw on the handle end. Americans know them better as "vise grips," but it's probably safe to say that if you don't know what I'm talking about on either score then you are not going to live life at a great deficit. **2** popular sexual position. This is a joke.

molly-coddled *adj* overly looked-after. Spoiled in a sort of possessive way: *He seemed very nice to start with but I think he's been rather molly-coddled by his mother.*

momentarily *adj* for a moment. Not to be confused with the U.S. definition, "in a moment." I was alerted to this by a Brit who heard a station announcement in Chicago that his train would be "stopping momentarily at platform 6" and was unsure as to whether he was supposed to take a running leap to get into it before it left.

moose *n* unattractive woman. Most often heard in post-drinking assessments: *Yeah, was a great night - we all got completely pissed and Bob ended up snogging a complete moose!*

moreish *adj* provoking of further consumption. I once wrote that you'd never find this word in a dictionary, but I had to change when someone pointed out to me that it was in the OED. I hate you all. It means something (usually food) which leads you to want more - *Jaffa Cakes*, *Jelly Babies* or dry roasted peanuts would be some good personal examples. It's rather light-hearted; you wouldn't go around describing heroin as *moreish*, whether it is or not.

motor *n* automobile. Derived from the time when all cars were known as "motor-cars."

motorway *n* freeway.

multi-storey car park *n* commercial car parking garage with, well, many floors. Americans call the same building a "parking ramp," "parking structure" or "parking deck," depending upon where they are in the country.

mum *n* mom. Brits do also use the word in the American sense of "quiet" (as in "keep mum about that") though maybe not as much in everyday speech as Americans. They'd probably say "schtum" instead.

munter *n* deeply unattractive woman. Pretty much equivalent to "dog" or "pig."

muppet *n* dimwit: *You've left the handbrake off, you muppet.*

N

naff *adj* tacky, ineffectual and generally crap. This could be a part of the reason why the French clothing firm *Naf Naf* recently pulled out of the U.K. It may derive from the 1960s gay slang language "Polari" in which it was used as an acronym for "Not Available For Fucking."

nancy *n* man who is either extremely effeminate, or homosexual. Or both. A rather derogatory term, and often conjoined into the phrase "nancy-boy."

nappy *n* diaper.

narked *adj* a bit annoyed; peeved. Brits do not use the word to refer to the act of reporting someone to the narcotics authorities.

nativity *n* crèche. Christian Christmas scene, usually featuring a plasticine baby Jesus lying in some grass. Normally made painstakingly over the course of several evenings by mothers of children who will take it to school and pass it off as their own work.

natter *n* engage in idle banter; chatter: *I thought she was busy getting ready to go out to dinner, but it turns out she'd spent the whole afternoon nattering to her mates.*

natty *adj* great; handy; cool: *I found this natty little device for stopping cables falling down the back of my desk.*

navvy *n* manual worker on roads or railways. It comes from the word "navigator," which was used to refer to people who dug canals, which were once called "navigations."

nearside *n* the side of a car closest to the kerb. The other side is the offside. Don't bother looking up "offside," because it's pretty much a copy-paste of this with one word changed. I'm lazy like that.

ned *n Scottish* unruly layabout youth. It is most likely derived from an acronym, "non-educated delinquent."

nick *v* **1** steal. Something you buy from a dodgy bloke over a pint has quite probably been nicked. In a strange paradox, if a person is described as *nicked*, it means they've been arrested and if a person is in *the nick*, they're in prison. **2** condition. Commonly used in the phrase "in good nick," the word *nick* refers to the sort of state of repair something is in: *Think I'll buy that car; it seems in pretty nice nick.*

niggle *n, adj* nag; pester. You might hear it in a context like: *He seemed okay, but I had a niggling doubt.*

nip 1 *v* quickly go and do something, very similar to "pop": *I'm just going to nip out for a minute.* **2** *n* chill: *There's a bit of a nip in the air*; *It's a bit nippy today.* And yes, the Brits do also use it to derogatorily refer to Japanese people, so the Pearl Harbour "nip in the air" jokes have probably been covered already.

nippy *adj* **1** irritating and irritable. Very similar to "stroppy." **2** cold. In a similar sort of a way to the word "chilly." **3** fast. Particularly in relation to cars. You might test-drive a car and relate back to your chums how nippy it was. Of course, if the salesman was a bit nippy you'd probably not drive it at all, or if it was a convertible and it was nippy outside.

nob *n* member of the aristocracy or person of importance. A contraction of "nobility."

nonce *n* child-molester. The term may originate from when sex offenders were admitted as "non-specified offenders" (thereby "non-specified" and thence "nonce") in the hope that they might not get the harsh treatment metered out to such convicts. It may also stand for "Not On Normal Courtyard Exercise" (meaning prisoners intended to keep separate from the rest). Either way, it featured prominently in the fine "Brasseye" spoof TV news programme where popular celebrities were duped into wearing T-shirts advocating "nonce-sense."

nosey parker *n* a person who takes a little bit too much interest in other people's goings on. Presumably "nosey" is related to putting one's nose in others' business, but heaven knows where the "parker" part came from.

nosh *n* food: *Right, the pub's shut, let's get some nosh.*

nought *n* *pron.* *"nawt"* the digit zero. It's an Old English word meaning "nothing" still used in northern regional English. Also occasionally used in the U.S., along with its more common American sibling, "aught."

noughts and crosses *n* tic-tac-toe.

nowt *n* *Northern England* nothing.

number plate *n* license plate. I already wrote about this under my entry for "registration" and I'll be damned if I'm writing any more.

numpty *n* *Scottish* idiot, in a friendly sort of a way: *You've parked in a disabled space, you numpty.*

nutter *n* someone with a screw loose. This applies to both the "insane" or "reckless" definitions, so a gentleman who scaled the Eiger naked and a chap who ate both of his parents could both validly be "nutters," albeit in slightly different ways.

O

och *interj Scottish* a general word of exclamation. Very Scottish. Groundskeeper Willie Scottish: *Och, yer jokin'!*

off-licence *n* liquor store. The term comes from the fact that the alcohol can be sold on the condition that it may only be drunk off the premises.

offside *n* the side of a car furthest from the kerb.

off one's onion *adj Northern England* crazy: *Some chap was dancing with cars in the street – I think he was off his onion!*

off one's trolley *adj* crazy: *Some chap was dancing with cars in the street – I think he was off his trolley!* Yes, I did just copy-paste the previous entry.

off one's rocker *adj* crazy: *Some chap was dancing with cars in the street – I think he was off his rocker!* And there I go again with the copy-paste. God, I love computers.

off one's tits *adj* high (on drugs): *I've no idea how she got up there, I was off my tits from about nine o'clock onwards. Perhaps she jumped?* Ah, you see, you thought I was going to copy-paste the previous entry again. Well, rest assured that I would have done had it meant the same thing.

oi *interj pron. "oy," as in "boy"* hey. General noise used to attract someone's attention. I can't really believe that an American being accosted with "oi" will be sitting there wondering whether that word means "faucet" or "yard," but I wouldn't like to feel this dictionary was too highbrow to be useful to people who had to be fed by their spouses with a spoon.

omnibus *n* **1** old-fashioned bus. This is a quaint word, dating back to the times when buses were open at the rear and had a conductor ready to meet you. An omnibus is essentially one step technologically forward of a tram. **2** concatenated episodes of a week's worth of television or radio series (typically soap operas) often screened at the weekends (also called "omnibus edition"). The Latin word "omnibus" means simply "for all," which could explain both of these etymologies. I'm just saying that because I can't be bothered checking either of them. I can't even be bothered checking the Latin - someone just told me it. For all I know it's Latin for pig-fucker.

on the blink *adj* not working right: *The television's been on the blink since we had the water-pistol fight.*

one *n* I. Rather antiquated and very British. You'd more likely hear your grandmother say "in my day, one didn't spit in the street" than your local crack dealer say "since Dave the Train got knocked off, one's had to raise one's prices."

one-off *n* something that only happens once. You might use it if you were selling your artwork or attempting to apologise for an affair with your secretary.

owt *n* anything. Rather northern-English: *Whatcha looking at me for? I didn't do owt!* It's recognised throughout the U.K. but it's a little unusual to use it.

P

P.A. *n* personal assistant. There is something of a new vogue in the U.K. for calling secretaries "personal assistants": *"Mr McDonald's secretary? No I certainly am not. Mr McDonald doesn't have a secretary. I am his pee-ay, thank you very much!"*

pantomime *n* light-hearted play, usually performed at Christmas and aimed at children. *Pantomimes* traditionally feature a man playing one of the lead female parts (the "pantomime dame"). There are a certain repertoire of standard pantomimes (*Jack and the Beanstalk, Cinderella, Aladdin* to name a few) and often reparatory groups will make up their own ones, either off the top of their thespian heads or based on other plays. The lead parts are usually played by second-rate soap-opera actors or half-dead theatrical-types. The whole genre is pretty crap, and essentially only exists so that children with special needs can feel normal.

pants 1 *n* underpants. What Americans call "pants," Brits call "trousers." **2** *interj* crap. A general derogatory word: *We went to see Andy playing in his band but to be honest they were pants.*

paraffin *n* Kerosene. The fuel used in some lamps, greenhouse heaters and such like. To confuse matters somewhat further, Americans call candle-wax "paraffin."

parky 1 *adj* cold; chilly; nippy. **2** *n* an abbreviation for Park-keeper. Despite my cavernous capacity for humour, try as I might I couldn't find any way to tie these in together.

pastille *n* a small candy. I don't know enough about candy to be more specific. A while ago the word was used to refer to cough drops, but now Brits largely call those "lozenges" or "throat sweets." The main use of the word now is in the branded chewy sweets made by Rowntree called *Fruit Pastilles*.

pasty *n pron. with a short "a," as in "hat"* meat or vegetable-filled pastries. Not to be confused with "pasties" (long "a," as in "face"), which in the U.S. are a flat pad designed to be put over the nipple to avoid it being too prominent. Or attach tassels to, depending on your fancy.

Patience *n* Solitaire. A card game played alone. I once wrote that the Brits would no doubt start calling it "solitaire" eventually, and some bastard half my age wrote to me to tell me that "mainly older people" call it "patience." So, sadly, I have to add here that this term is used by "mainly older people." This reminds me of the time my mother came home in tears when a boy scout had tried to help her across the road. Rather oddly, we Brits also call another game "Solitaire." Just go and look it up like a man.

pavement *n* sidewalk. Brits call the part that cars drive on "Tarmac." I wonder how many holidaymakers have been run over as a result of this confusion. Well, probably none really. I digress. Historically, "sidewalk" is in fact an old, now-unused British English word meaning exactly what the Americans take it to mean.

pear-shaped *adj* gone wrong. Usually it's meant in a rather jovial sense, in a similar way to the American expression "out of kilter" or "off kilter": *Well, I was supposed to have a civilised dinner with my mates but we had a few drinks and it all went a bit pear-shaped.* You would be less likely to see: *Well, she went in for the operation but the transplant organ's been rejected and the doctor says it's all gone a bit pear-shaped.* Possible derivations involve glass-blowing or hot-air ballooning. Separately.

pecker *n* penis. A common misconception is that, to Brits, this means "chin" - hence the phrase "keep your pecker up." Sorry folks, but in the U.K. "pecker" means exactly the same thing as it does in the U.S. The phrase "keep your pecker up" is probably derived

from a time when a "pecker" was simply a reference to a bird's beak and encouraged keeping your head held high. I understand that the word became a euphemism for "penis" after the poet Catullus used it to refer to his love Lesbia's pet sparrow in a rather suggestive poem which drew some fairly blatant parallels.

peckish *adj* hungry. Absolutely nothing to do with "pecker." Only a little hungry, mind, not ravenous - you wouldn't hear people on the news talking about refugees who'd tramped across mountains for two weeks and were as a result a little peckish.

peculiar *adj* unique: *These street signs are peculiar to Birmingham.* Because Brits also share the more conventional meaning ("unusual"), it does slightly imply that. If street signs can really be that unusual. Also applies to things other than street signs.

Pelican crossing *n* pedestrian crossing. An area of the road, marked with black and white stripes, where traffic lights stop cars so that pedestrians can cross. A contraction of "PEdestrian LIght CONtrolled crossing." Yes, I know that would be "pelicon." People were stupid back then.

pensioner *n* senior. Quite simply someone who is drawing their pension, i.e. over the age of 65. Brits also use the acronym OAP, meaning "Old-Aged Pensioner."

Perspex *n* Plexiglas. A sort of plastic equivalent of glass. Perspex is a brand name of the acrylic company

Lucite. Their advertising literature probably has all sorts of fancy terms in it about covalent bonds and stress ratings, and perhaps doesn't even use the phrase "a sort of plastic equivalent of glass." Unless maybe they have a layman's FAQ at the end.

petrol *n* gas. An abbreviation of "petroleum," much like "gas" is an abbreviation of "gasoline."

phone box *n* phone booth. One of those boxes with a telephone in it that used to be commonplace but are dying out somewhat now that everyone has a mobile phone. The government still erect a few to give errant youths have something to vandalise in the long winter evenings and prostitutes somewhere to advertise. Of course, they all do that via email now.

phut *adj pron. "fuht"* **gone-** Something which has breathed its last, expired. It is an ex-something: *We ended up stuck watching BBC2 because the television remote control had gone phut.*

pickle *n* **1** a sort of brown, strongly flavoured blobby mass that people put in sandwiches. I'm really not very sure what it's made of. Pickled something, one can only hope. **2** any sort of pickled cucumber or gherkin (universal).

piece *n. Scottish* packed lunch. Quintessentially Scottish: *Will ye be coming for lunch, Willie? / Nah, ah've brought ma piece.*

pig's ear *n* a mess; a poor job: *We paid the guy from down the road to come and finish painting the fence, but he made a complete pig's ear of*

it. Probably comes from the phrase "you can't make a sow's purse from a pig's ear."

pikey *n adj* white trash. It's an old English word meaning "gipsy," but nowadays *pikey* is also applied to people in possession of track suits, Citroen Saxos with eighteen-inch wheels and under-car lighting, and pregnant fifteen-year-old girlfriends.

pillock *n* idiot. You could almost decide having read this dictionary that any unknown British word is most likely to mean "idiot." And you could almost be right. The Brits have so many because different ones sound better in different sentences. *Pillock* is likely a contraction of the 16th century word "pillicock," which was used to refer to the male member.

pinch *v* steal. A contributor of mine told me that her father got anything but the reaction he expected when in New Orleans he asked a friend if he could *pinch* their date for a dance. The Brits do not share the American usage of "pinch," to mean arresting someone.

pint *n* the standard U.K. measure of beer - equivalent to 0.568 litres in new money or twenty ounces in American money. It is normally possible to buy a half-pint instead of a pint, but doing so will mar you for life in the eyes of your peers. Drinking half-pints of beer is generally seen as the liquid equivalent of painting your fingernails and mincing. At some point in history (no idea when) a British king (not sure which one) elected to raise tax on beer but upon discovering that he needed an act of parliament to change the tax, he instead changed the size of the pint (which only required a royal edict). The smaller sixteen-ounce American pint, therefore actually represents the original size of the British pint. As you can see I've not researched this at all. I just wrote down what someone told me. There are many times in my life when I'm forced to make a simple choice between the real truth and a funny story.

pips *n* seeds. The little seeds in the middle of fruit guaranteed to get stuck in your teeth.

pish *n, v Scottish* piss. It can be used not only to refer to urine/urination, but also as a mild sort of swear word, similar to "crap."

piss-artist *n* useless layabout. The .com must have gone, but I'm too scared to check. Have you ever played that game where you pick a .com and bet amongst your friends as to whether it's a porn site or not. I bet you're sitting there thinking that sounds like a stupid game, but let me get you started. turkishdelight.com? You're wondering, aren't you?

pissed *adj* drunk. Brits do not use it alone as a contraction of "pissed off," which means that Americans saying things like "I was really pissed with my boss at work today" leaves Brits wide-eyed. **go out on the** - venture out drinking. **taking the** - poking fun at someone. May well be a throwback to the U.S. use of the word.

pitch *n* an area of land. Almost exclusively used in reference to a playing field (Brits say "football *pitch*" rather than "football field"), but can also mean an area allocated to a trader, e.g. in a market.

plasticine *n* modeling clay. It's a particular brand in the U.K. but no Brit will ever have heard of any others.

plaster *n* Band-Aid. **sticking** - a more old-fashioned word meaning the same. Both British and American English share the term *plastered* to mean that you are wildly under the influence of alcohol.

plimsolls *n* light canvas shoes with rubber soles. A rather antiquated shoe, and therefore an equally antiquated word. Your grandmother may refer to your trainers as *plimsolls*, but that doesn't mean you should too.

Plod *n* the Police: *You climb over the fence and I'll keep an eye out for Plod.* The word derives from a character in Enid Blyton's *Noddy* books named PC Plod.

plonker *adj* idiot. I'm tempted to write a Dictionary of British Insults. Also (rarely) used to refer to one's penis. Or someone else's, if you don't have one. Or if you do have one, but you're trying to refer to someone else's and not your own. I'm tempted to also write a Dictionary of British Words For Penis. A future bestseller; keep an eye out. Not that eye.

plus-fours *n* an awful item of clothing which consists of sort-of-dungarees which stop at the knee.

Whilst popular in pre-World-War Britain, plus-fours these days are firmly in the realms of brightly-colours golfers or inbreds.

po-faced *adj* glum; long-faced: *I bumped into Sheena in the newsagent this afternoon - she looked mighty po-faced about something.* As well as being a useful word for people who want to win at Scrabble by memorising stupid goddamned two-letter words and then sitting there looking all smug about them even thought they don't know what they mean, "Po" is an abbreviation for "chamber pot" (an old-fashioned bed-pan).

polo-neck *n, adj* turtle-neck. A style of sweater in which the neck runs right up to the chin; far enough up to cover even the most adventurous of love-bites.

polythene *n* polyethylene. The plastic-type stuff that plastic bags are made of.

ponce 1 *n* man who is pretentious in an effeminate manner. "Ponces" (quite often referred to using the phrase *perfume ponce*) tend to grown their hair quite long and talk loudly into their mobile phones while sitting at the traffic lights in their convertible Porsche. Describing a place as *poncy* would imply that these sorts of punters made up the bulk of its clientele. **2** *v* scrounge: *Can I ponce a fag off you?* Apparently the word originally meant living off the earnings of prostitution. Please look up "fag" now, before I cause some sort of ghastly mistake.

pong *n* bad smell. My maths teacher at school, Mr Benzies, also taught my uncle, who was fifteen or so years older than me. My uncle told me that in his day Mr Benzies was known unanimously as "Pongo Benzies" because "wherever he goes, the pong goes." If you're reading this, Mr Benzies, please remember that I'm just relating what my uncle said, and I didn't necessarily actually call you that, or try and get the rest of the year to call you it too.

poof *n* homosexual. A mildly derogatory term for a homosexual - mild in the sense that homosexuals might use it themselves. Although based upon that I could easily say that "nigger" was a mildly derogatory term for an African American. **poofy** effeminate. An episode of Magnum PI, the U.S. detective show, features Magnum himself describing Zeus and Hercules as "poofy names for attack dogs." Whilst in the U.S. this is taken to mean "fancy," in the U.K. it would quite definitely mean "homosexual."

poofter *n* a simple derivation of "poof," with exactly the same meaning.

porkies *n* lies. From Cockney rhyming slang "pork pies" / "lies."

Portakabin *n* a sort of prefabricated hut, most often used as temporary offices on a building-site. A portable cabin, if you will. *Portakabin* is a U.K. trademark.

posh *adj* upper-class. Your aunt Mabel might be *posh* because she lives in a large country house, or your dad's new Mercedes might have seemed a little bit too *posh* for him. It's not rude, but it's not really particularly complimentary either. The term originates from the acronym "Port Out, Starboard Home," which referred to customers travelling on boats between the U.K. and India who had chosen to have the more expensive shaded berths on both the outward and return journeys. **posh wank** masturbation performed whilst wearing a condom (male-specific, one would imagine).

post *n, v* mail. Brits don't mail things, they *post* them. Their mail is delivered by a *postman* (one word). And, umm, he works for an organisation called the *Royal Mail*. It's pretty much the reverse of how these two words are used in America.

postgraduate *n* grad student. Someone who's finished their university degree and, on the sudden realisation that they might have to actually get a job, has instead leapt enthusiastically into a PhD, a Masters, or some such other form of extended lunch-break.

Pot Noodle *n* Cup-o-Noodle. Little pots of noodles, upon which you simply pour boiling water to the "fill level" and lo, all of a sudden you have a perfectly delicious and nutritious meal for one. One student, one overworked employee or one neglected pensioner, normally. I don't think it mentions that on the pot.

potholing *n* caving; spelunking. The sport that involves leaping down holes in the ground. I'm sure that, in a special way, it's fun. Brits do still refer to chunks that are missing from the road as *potholes*, in the same way as Americans.

potplant *n* plant in a pot. Not a cannabis plant. Well, it could be, but more than likely it isn't.

potty *adj* loopy; nuts. A fairly light-hearted term for someone who's losing their marbles a bit. Brits do also share the American meaning, where it refers to a plastic child's toilet bowl. Not that plastic children probably ever need the toilet.

poxy *adj* crappy; third-rate. Presumably derived in some way from when horrible things were described as being ridden with a pox.

pram *n* baby carriage. An abbreviation for the rather Victorian and now largely unused term "perambulator."

prang *n* fender-bender. An event towards the more sedate end of car accidents - you're unlikely to hear on the news that fourteen people were killed in a multi-car *prang* and ensuing fireball on Wednesday evening.

prat *n* idiot: *I met my sister's boyfriend the other day and he seems like a complete prat.* Derived from a time when the word was slang for your posterior (in a similar way to the more contemporaneous "arse") from whence, interestingly, came the peculiarly American word "pratfall" (a fall on one's behind).

prawn *n* the least powerful piece on a chess board. OK, I lied. It's a shrimp.

prefect *n* a school-child who, having done particularly well academically or on the sports field, is allowed to perform such glorious tasks as making sure everyone behaves properly in the lunch queue, tidying up after school events and showing new pupils around at the weekends. As you may have guessed, I was never a *prefect*. Bitter? Me?

prep school *n* boarding school for children from ages eight to thirteen.

presenter *n* anchor (the person, not the nautical device). In the U.K., presenters of news programmes are known as *presenters* rather than "anchors." Likewise, the Brits have *co-presenters* instead of "co-anchors," a term which almost caused my boss to regurgitate his drink during a U.S. business trip when he heard it as "co-wanker."

pub *n* bar. An abbreviation for "public house." However, in my experience, British *pubs* are generally far more sociable than American bars. While you would go into a *pub* to have a pleasant lunch with your family or one or two sociable beers with a couple of friends, you'd only go into a bar in order to get blind drunk and then start a fight or have sex with something.

public school *n* I wrote a whole chapter about this earlier on, and I'm not writing it again. It begins on page 22.

pudding *n* dessert: *If you keep spitting at your grandfather like that you're going to bed without any pudding!* Brits do also use the word in the same sense as Americans do (*Christmas pudding, rice pudding,* etc). The word "dessert" is used in the U.K. but really only in restaurants, never in the home. To complicate things further, the Brits have main meal dishes which are described as *pudding* - *black pudding* and *white pudding.* These are revolting subsistence foods from the dark ages made with offal, ground oatmeal, dried pork and rubbish from the kitchen floor. The difference between the black and white *puddings* is that the black one contains substantial quantities of blood. This, much like haggis, is one of those foodstuffs that modern life has saved us from but that people insist on dredging up because it's a part of their "cultural heritage." Bathing once a year and shitting in a bucket was a part of your cultural heritage too, you know. At least be consistent.

pukka *interj* the genuine article; good stuff: *I was a bit dubious when they were selling Levis for twenty quid, but I reckon they're pukka.* It is derived from the Hindi word "pakka," meaning "substantial," and made it to the U.K. via the Colonies.

pull *v* hook up. The art of attracting the opposite sex: *You're not going to pull with breath smelling like that.* **on the pull** a less proactive version of "sharking." Single males and females are almost all on the pull but will deny it fervently and pretend to be terribly surprised when eventually it pays off.

pump *n* gym shoes. A rather antiquated term. The confusion arises because in the U.S., it means high heels or stilettos.

puncture 1 *n* flat tire. In the U.K., *puncture* is used to describe the offending tire itself rather than just the hole in it: *We had to pull over because we got a puncture.* **2** infraction (universal).

punter *n* guy. A punter is usually a customer of some sort (the word originally meant someone who was placing bets at a racecourse), but this need not be the case. Because of the word's gambling roots, punters are regarded slightly warily and shouldn't necessarily be taken at face value: *When I came out of the tube station there was some punter there saying his car had broken down and he needed five quid to put petrol in it.* Because American Football isn't very popular in the U.K., Brits are unaware of the role of a punter on a football team (though they do share the everyday definition of the word "punt").

purse *n* money-purse. A little bag that women generally keep money in. Brits call anything larger than a money-purse a "handbag."

pushchair *n* baby buggy; stroller. A device in which a small child is pushed along by an obliging parent. The American term "buggy" is squeezing its way into everyday use in the U.K.

put paid to *v* put an end to: *We were going to have a picnic in the park but the weather put paid to that.*

Q

quay *n pron. "key"* the place in a docks where boats are loaded and unloaded. The word exists in American English, but the British pronunciation can cause blank stares.

queue *n, v, pron. "cue"* line. This doesn't really help the definition at all, as a line could be any number of things. A pencil line? A railway line? A line of Charlie? A line dancer? As a result of this potentially dangerous confusion, a word was developed by some British word-scientists to separate this particular line from all the others. A *queue* is a line of people. To *queue* is to be one of those *queuing* in the *queue*. The word means "tail" in French, and is used in the same context. Americans do in fact use the word, but only in the "you're third in the queue" type telephone call waiting systems.

quid *n* pound (currency). *Quid* is to "pound" what "buck" is to "dollar." The word is very widely recognised and socially acceptable but informal - you could quite easily say: "Well, they offered me ten thousand quid for the car" but you wouldn't hear any BBC announcers reporting "The government today authorised a ten million quid increase in health service funding." This perhaps says more about the BBC than this one particular word, but I digress.

quite *n* kind of; sort of: *What did you think of Jean's new boyfriend? / Hmm, yeah, I suppose he was quite nice.* This is something of a tough one because Brits will also use *quite*, in the same way as Americans, to mean "very." The only real way to determine exactly which type of *quite* is being used is to look at how expressive the word that follows it is. If it's a word like "perfect" or "delicious" then it's being used the positive way; if it's a word like "nice" or "pleasant" then it's negative.

quim *n* female genitalia. Rather antiquated. The person who asked about the word also asked me: "As bad as American "cunt" or "twat"? Or more akin to the mellower "pussy"? Would Britwomen themselves ever use the term to refer to their own anatomy with other women friends? Would men ever use it to refer to women in a derogatory way?" No, Yes, No, Yes. Hope that helps.

R

railway *n* railroad. Can't think of anything witty.

randy *adj* horny. One way of ensuring that Brits laugh at American sitcoms is to put someone in the program called Randy. Sentences such as "Hello, I'm Randy" have us doubled up on the sofa.

rat-arsed *adj* exceedingly drunk. Also abbreviated as simply *ratted*. Possibly derived from a time when dead rats would be dangled in cider vats to give them extra flavour. At least, according to the person who told me that.

rawl plug *n* moly bolt. If you don't know what either of these things is, rest assured that your life may continue.

razz *v* vomit: *Well, yeah, we were having a great time until Phil razzed down the back of the sofa and they made us all go home.*

the razz an evening spent out drinking. Both Americans and Brits use the term "razzing" to describe teasing someone.

reckon *adv* believe to be true. It's still perfectly acceptable in the U.K. to say "I reckon" this, that or the other: *We're going to get a taxi to the airport but Dan reckons we're still not going to make it.* The term is still used in the Southern U.S. but regarded with disdain by snobby northerners who believe it can only be uttered whilst chewing a piece of straw and leaning on a gate.

registration *n* licence plate. While Americans can have anything they fancy on theirs, and they bear little pictures of sunny beaches and legends like "Ohio - The Flour Biscuit State" and such, the Brits have slightly more plain affairs and less choice about what goes on them. Well, no choice at all, in point of fact. As the government changed their systems of number/letter combinations a good few times, however, there is a lively secondary market in plates that look like they say something.

return ticket *adj* round-trip ticket. As you probably know, it just means that you're planning on coming home again.

reverse charges *n, v* call collect. Nothing to do with cars or batteries.

revise *v* study: *I can't go out tonight, my mum says I've got to stay home revising.* All the other meanings of the word remain the same.

ride *v* screw (in a sexual sense): *Jim's not coming out tonight, I think he's staying at home riding that fat bird from the pub.*

ring *n, v* call (as in telephone): *You coming out later? / Dunno... give me a ring.* A relic from the days when telephones actually rang and didn't bleep, vibrate or send you e-mail.

rocket *n* arugula.

rodger *v* hump. *Rodgering* is, well, shagging, and tends to also imply shagging of the arse variety. And I know it's a name, but then so's Randy. I used to work with a gentleman named Roger Tallboys.

romp *v* the loving act of procreation. It's a bit rough-and-ready - you would be much more likely to have a *romp* with your secretary on top of the photocopier than you would with your wife of thirty years in the marital bed. Not you personally, these are just examples.

ropey *adj* iffy; something which isn't in as good as state as it might be. It might be you with a hangover; your ex-girlfriend or the car you bought from someone in the pub last week: *I can't come into work today - I'm feeling a bit ropey* or: *We took a look over the plans but to be honest they looked a bit ropey.*

roundabout *n* traffic circle; rotary. The device put into the road as a snare for learner drivers and foreigners. Everyone has to drive around in a circle until they see their selected exit road, at which point they must fight through the other traffic on the roundabout in a valiant attempt to leave it. *Roundabouts* do exist in the U.S. (predominantly in Massachusetts) but in the U.K. they're all over the place - there is no such thing as a four-way-stop.

row *n pron. like "cow,"* rather than *"sew"* an argument. More likely a domestic argument than a fight outside a pub. Unless you have an unusually vicious spouse or a girly pub.

rozzer *n* policeman. Even more esoteric than the good old English "bobby," most British people will never have heard of this term. It may come from a P. G. Wodehouse book, and is certainly mentioned in the Paul McCartney song "London Town."

rubber *n* eraser. Be very, very careful. Limies visiting the United States are urged by the government to write this translation on the back of their hands and not to wash until they leave.

rubbish *n* trash; garbage. Everyday waste.

rucksack *n* backpack. One of those bags you wear over your shoulder on two straps (or one, if you want to look misguidedly fashionable). The word is used in the U.S. armed forces specifically to mean a framed pack, but in the U.K. it means any sort of backpack.

S

sack *v* dismiss; fire: *Well, I pretty much knew I was getting sacked as soon as they walked in and saw me on the photocopier.* Comes from a time when you were given a sack into which to put the contents of your desk. In the U.S., the term "given the sack" is used sporadically, but not the word *sack* alone as a verb.

salad cream *n* A mixture of mayonnaise and vinegar often put on salads. Perhaps unsurprisingly.

saloon *n* sedan. The cars that, well, aren't estates or sports cars. The kind your dad and the dentist have. They are called *saloons* in the U.K. because they usually have wooden swing doors, spittoons and people tend to burst into them waving a gun and saying something about the car not being big enough for two of us. Them. Us. I see why people hate learning English.

samey *adj* similar: *We looked at ten flats that afternoon but they were all just a bit samey.*

sarnie *n abbrev* sandwich. A little bit slang-ish - you won't find a "lightly toasted roast beef sarnie served on a fresh bed of rocket" in your average poncy restaurant.

savoury *n* non-dessert food. Food such as potatoes, bread and meat are *savouries*. Things like ice cream and meringues are "sweets," which is defined elsewhere in this fine work. Probably further on, as it's supposed to be in alphabetical order.

scarper *v* run away. Usually from the scene of some sort of unpleasant incident in which you were a part: *I saw some kids out the window writing all over my car in spray paint but by the time I got there they'd scarpered.* It may be derived from the Cockney rhyming slang "Scappa Flow" / "go." Scappa Flow is a large natural harbour on an island north of Scotland where the British naval fleet was kept during World War One. All this extra information provided free of charge.

school *n* pre-university education - in the U.K. they call university, well, university.

schtum *adj pron.* *"shtoom"* silent. Only really used in the phrase "keep schtum," meaning "keep your mouth shut" in the U.K. It is derived from the German adjective "stumm," meaning being either unable or unwilling to speak.

scone *n pron.* *"sk-awn,"* not *"sk-own"* biscuit. Sort of. A quintessentially British foodstuff, *scones* are somewhere between a cake and a subsistence food. The

British word is creeping into the U.S. via coffee shops. Can a word creep?

Scotch a contraction of the word "Scottish," this is now only used in the context of foodstuffs (and even then really just *Scotch eggs*), and whisky – Brits refer to anything else as being "Scottish." So those from Scotland aren't *Scotch* people; they are *Scottish* people. If they were *Scotch* people, they would be made primarily from whisky. Oh, wait…

Scotch egg *n* a somewhat peculiar delicacy - a hard-boiled egg wrapped in sausage meat and coated in breadcrumbs. My mother used to put them in my packed lunch every day for school.

scouser *n* someone from Liverpool. Perhaps more accurately someone with a Liverpool accent. The word comes from "lobscouse," which was a dish sailors ate, much like Irish Stew - sailors were known as "lobscousers" and the port of Liverpool ended up tagged with the same word. Further back still, the original word may have come from Norway, where today "Lapp Skews" are stewed strips of reindeer meat. Or perhaps it comes from Bangladesh, where "Lump Scouts" is a rare dish made from boy-scouts and served at Christmas. Or from a parallel universe, almost identical to ours, where *scousers* are people from Birmingham.

scrap *n, v, adj* junk. While Americans have junkyards and put junk on junk-heaps, Brits have *scrapyards* and *scrap-heaps*, upon which they put *scrap*.

scrote *n* scum. Someone generally about as low in one's esteem as a person could be. It may be an abbreviation of "scrotum" which, now I think about it, could perhaps be the derivation of "scum." I have a small pain in my sc'um, m'lord.

scrubber *n* another not overly complimentary word for a young lady of loose moral fibre.

scrummy *adj* delicious. I believe that this is a childish amalgamation of "yummy" and "scrumptious": *This jelly and ice-cream is scrummy!*

Scrumpy *n* strong alcoholic cider. While traditionally the word refers to home-brewed cider (*scrumping* being the stealing of apples), it has more recently become associated with a high-alcohol brand named *Scrumpy Jack*. Don't go near the stuff. I drank some at university one evening and all sorts of bad things happened.

scupper *v* obstruct; stymie: *We were planning on having a party but then my folks arrived home early and scuppered that.* The term derives from seafaring, where the *scupper* is a drain designed to allow water to flow overboard from the deck. To be *scuppered* is to be hit by a wave large enough to knock you into this drain. Of course, it could also derive from the more obvious seafaring source where *scuppering* something is sinking it, but hey. I make a lot of these up on the spot.

Sellotape *n Scotch tape. Sellotape* (a contraction of "cellophane tape") is the name of the largest manufacturer of sticky tape in the U.K.

septic *n* American: *Hey, did you hear Bob had moved to New York and married a septic?* From Cockney rhyming slang "septic tank" / "yank," where "yank" is in turn used in the U.K. to mean "American." If you don't believe me, look it up, but I have to warn you that I also wrote that definition. The Australians use the same term and have further abbreviated *septic* to "seppo."

serviette *n* napkin. The thing you put in your lap to block the path of food falling onto your clothes.

shag 1 *v* lay (sexual). Usually refers to the act of intercourse itself, except when used by a bloke giving his mates the details about what happened with that tidy bird he pulled in the club the night before. In this case, the term *shag* should be interpreted to mean anything between a peck on the cheek and a punch in the face. Brits find very amusing the use of the word "shag" in the U.S. to refer to certain dances. **2** *adj* **shagged** tired. In much the same way as most other humping words can be used: *Spent the whole day hiking and now I'm completely shagged.*

shambolic *adj* in complete disarray, unorganised; in shambles. You might use it to refer to your aunt Gertrude's octogenarian hairdo or the Russian army's method of ending hostage situations. If I was ever to give one piece of advice to someone wanting independence for

their part of the U.S.S.R. or keen to highlight a particular cause to the Russian government, I'd suggest not taking hostages. If you do so, the Russians give you a couple of days of negotiations, throw in a bit of food so you feel you've got your money's worth and then on about day three they massacre you and all of your hostages using some devastating new method they're trying for the first time.

shandy *n* an alcoholic mix of lager and (British) lemonade. Usually 90% lager and 10% lemonade, and generally drunk by people convinced that they can get as drunk as a skunk on *shandy* and still be fine to drive the car. *Shandy* has also given us such retail gems as *Top Deck*, a canned drink which contains not only the cheapest lemonade money can buy, but rounds it off nicely with a dash of the grottiest beer available west of the Himalaya.

shark *v*, hunt members of the opposite sex, with copulation in mind. The easiest way to spot someone who is *sharking* is to watch their friends, who will every so often hold one hand just above their head like a fin just to make the point. The difference between *sharking* and being "on the pull" is that *sharking* is slightly more proactive. If you're on the pull you won't say no; if you're *sharking* you won't take no for an answer. I was once told that "shark" in U.S. slang is, erm, a sexual technique. I then tried and failed to describe the act itself in polite terms, and have subsequently given up.

shat *n* the past-participle of "shit" – this also exists in the U.S. but is in much more common usage in the U.K.: *That pigeon just shat on my car!*

shattered *adj* extremely tired; emotionally devastated. You could be *shattered* by the death of your dear mother or a good invigorating jog. Experiencing both simultaneously would leave you *shattered* in two different ways at once, and probably reasonably angry. Can there really be a God if the world contains this much suffering? No, probably not.

Shilling *n* a pre-decimalisation U.K. unit of currency - worth five pence.

shimmy *n, v* deft evasive manoeuvre: *The bull went straight for him but Mike shimmied out of the way.*

shirt-lifter *n* homosexual man. A slightly archaic term. It may come from a time when shirts had longer tails and, well, posterial access required some lifting. Don't pretend to me you don't know what I'm talking about.

shirty *adj* testy; irritable. May have originated in a time when people used to take off their shirts to fight and so "getting shirty" meant that you were preparing to thrash a rotten scoundrel to within an inch of his pitiful life.

shite *n* shit. The only plausible reason I can think of for this word's existence at all is that it has more rhyming potential for football songs. Perhaps soon we'll have the word "shitove," giving Whitney

Houston and her cohorts further opportunities to over-use the word "love" in their drivelly good-for-nothing pop songs.

shop *n* store. What Americans call "shops," the Brits call "workshops" or "garages."

sick *n* vomit. Brits call the act of vomiting *being sick*, and vomit itself *sick*: *Gah! There's sick all down the back of my shirt!* Like Americans they do use the noun to also mean "unwell," so saying "I am sick" does not translate to "I am vomit."

sickie *n* a day off work elicited by feigning illness: *I'm going to take a sickie tomorrow and go to the zoo!*

skallywag *n* rascal. A young tearaway. A bit of an antiquated term.

skanky *adj* disgusting. Describing something or someone as *skanky* would imply that they haven't been cleaned in quite some time. Brits do not use the word "skank" to refer to a prostitute.

skinfull *n* the amount of alcohol necessary to make one clearly inebriated. If you have a *skinfull* at lunch, you'll be less likely to go back to the office and more likely to see whether you could urinate as high as the top of the "M" in the McDonalds logo.

skint *adj* broke. The position of having no money: *Dave refused to give me any petrol money - was moaning on the whole time about how skint he was.*

skip *n* dumpster. It's odd that something as revolting should develop such a pleasant name. The dumpster was invented by a man called Skip Mandible. This is a lie.

skirting board *n* baseboard. The little wooden bit of edging that goes around the bottom of the walls in your house so that when you stub your toe you don't put your foot through the plasterboard.

skive *v, n* play hookie: *We've got chemistry this afternoon but I'm just going to skive as I can't be arsed.* Differs from "playing hookie" in that it may also be used as a noun: *Our team meetings are basically a complete skive.*

slag 1 *v* **-off** have a go at; pick on: *We gave Charlie a right slagging off when he turned up four hours late and covered in toothpaste.* **2** *n* slut. A woman with very loose morals: *I don't think much of Derek's bird... Ian thinks she's a slag.*

slaphead *n* bald person: *Have you noticed that Charlie's becoming something of a slaphead? Lucky for him he's on the tall side.*

slapper *n* slut. Person on the prowl for anything they can get. Anything. The word is applied more often to females, arguably because it is a built-in function of blokes and doesn't deserve a separate word. *Slappers* wander around the dance floor looking for the drunkest blokes and then, when they've found them, woo them by dancing backwards into them "accidentally." They are invariably spotted at the end of an evening telling the bouncer how lonely they are and trying to sit on his knee.

slash *v* **have a-** urinate. Its usage is more appropriate to punters in the pub than middle-aged ladies at a Tupperware party.

sleeper *n* railroad tie. The very large blocks of wood which go between the rails and the ground on a section of railway line.

sleeping policeman *n* speed-bump. The name probably derives from a time when narcoleptic policemen were employed to slow down traffic.

slip-road *n* on-ramp/off-ramp. A road that runs parallel to a major one, allowing you to gain or lose speed safely while joining or leaving the main road.

Smarties *n* small sugar-coated chocolate candies, not entirely dissimilar to chocolate *M&Ms*. Not related at all to the American candy product of the same name, which in the U.K. is known as *Fizzers*.

smashing *adj* great. Contrary to appearances, something which is *smashing* is a good thing rather than a bad one: *Mum, I had a smashing time playing football in the park!* It may be derived from the Gaelic phrase "is math sin," which means "that's good."

smeg *n* generic swear word based upon the word "smegma." Also a popular German kitchen equipment manufacturer, who are no doubt in the process of changing their name. Popularised (and most likely invented) by Rob Naylor, who created the *Red Dwarf* book and television series.

snap *n* ditto; me too: *Do you know, I think I slept with that guy in my* *first year of university. / Oh god! Snap!*

Snakes and Ladders *n* chutes and ladders. The simple board game in which you roll dice and, depending on which square you land on, you can go whizzing further up the board on ladders or slide down the board on snakes.

snog *v* make out; french kiss: *I had a couple too many beers and ended up snogging the bouncer.*

soap *n* bar of soap. To a Brit, *soap* is specifically the soap you use to wash yourself in the bath, not something you'd use to wash clothes or dishes.

sod 1 *n, v, adj* generic word signifying displeasure. Attached to any word or phrase it has the immediate effect of making it derogatory. **Sod off** get lost. **sod you** bite me. **sod it** damn it; forget it. **old sod** old git, etc, etc. Use at will - it has a friendly tone to it and is unlikely to get you into trouble. **2** *n* a lump of turf (universal).

soldiers *n* strips of bread meant for dipping into a boiled egg. And yes, Brits also use the word to describe people who are in the army. To the best of my knowledge this duality of meaning has never caused any enormous problems.

solicitor *n* lawyer. In the U.K. it has nothing (well, on one level at least) to do with prostitutes or door-to-door salesmen.

Solitaire *n* a game played alone on a sort of four-pointed-star board full of pegs in little holes, where the idea is to remove pegs by jumping other pegs over the top of them,

ultimately with the intention of ending up with a single peg left on the board in the middle. Traditionally, the Brits refer to card games one plays alone as "patience" rather than "solitaire" but Microsoft has gone a fair way to changing that.

sorted *adj* sorted-out: *You've got it? Great. Sorted.* I am ninety-nine percent sure that this originated in a drugs context, a view only strengthened by the existence of a *Pulp* song entitled *Sorted for 'E's and Whiz.*

spanner 1 *n* wrench. 2 *adj* A very mild friendly insult: *Bob'll be a bit late; the spanner left his phone in a taxi.*

spare *adj* at one's wits end; mad: *I've been trying to get this working all morning and it's driving me spare!*

speedo *n* abbreviation for "speedometer."

spotted dick *n* a sponge cake with raisins in it. And yes, the Brits do use "dick" to mean the same thing Americans do.

sprog *n* small child. My father used to refer to myself and my brothers as *"Sprog* One," *"Sprog* Two" and *"Sprog* Three." Perhaps that says more about my family than the English language. At least I got to be *Sprog* One. Were my father Australian he might have chosen some different phrasing as to an Aussie "sprog" is what the rest of the world calls semen.

spunk 1 *n* semen. 2 someone with a bit of drive (universal).

squash *n. v* cordial; diluted fruit drink. It's a little outdated - you'd be more likely to find your grandmother offering you "lemon squash" than you would your children. The vegetable that Americans call a "squash," Brits call a "marrow."

squiffy *adj* pear-shaped. Pretty much anything that's gone wrong.

stabilisers *n* training wheels. The little extra set of wheels that your parents put on your bicycle to stop you from falling off all the time when you're learning to ride. My parents never got any... I think they secretly enjoyed watching me injure myself in the name of learning.

stag night *n* bachelor party. The groom's pre-wedding lads'-night-out party. It generally involves drinking as much alcohol as possible and trying to do something embarrassing to the husband-to-be. This is great fun for all of the groom's buddies, but less fun for the groom as he almost inevitably wakes up the next morning completely naked and tied to a lamppost somewhere in a foreign country. Brides secretly like *stag nights* because it gives them a good excuse for refusing to let their husbands see their friends again.

starter *n* appetizer. The dish you eat prior to your main meal.

steady on *interj* whoa; hold your horses. Almost always followed by an exclamation mark: *OK, that does it, I'm resigning! / Steady on!*

sterling *adj* good/great: *That main course was sterling stuff.*

sticking plaster *n* Somewhat antiquated version of "plaster." See "plaster" for definition. I can't be bothered copy-pasting.

stockings *n* tights. I think. I don't wear a lot of women's underwear. Well, there was that one time.

stodgy *adj* sticky; reluctant to change. Could apply equally easily to people (*Everyone else was very eager except Bob, who was being decidedly stodgy about it*) or substances (*the soup looked nice but it turned out to be stodgy as hell*).

stone 1 *n* unit of measure (14lbs). Only really used when measuring the weight of people. **2** *n* pit. The large hard seeds inside fruit (peaches, olives and the like).

stonking *adj* enormous: *When I finally woke up, I had a stonking hangover and my wallet had vanished. And I appeared not to be in my bed at home, but under a park bench.*

straight away *interj* right now: *Once you buy our fine credit card, you can start to make purchases with it straight away!*

Strimmer *n* Weed-Whacker. A gardening device held at waist level, with a piece of nylon cord near the ground which whips around to slice the stems of errant plants and the toenails of inebriated pensioners.

stroppy *adj* unreasonable; unfairly grumpy. *Stroppy* people shout at shop assistants who don't know where the tomato puree is and, because they're being paid £2/hr, ought not to be expected to.

subway *n* underground pedestrian walkway. Built to enable you to cross the road safely, urinate or inject heroin. Brits do not call the London underground train system the "subway." They call it the "underground."

sultana *n* golden raisin. Vine-dried green grape.

sun cream *n* sunscreen.

supper *n Scottish* takeaway meal served with (British) chips. When dish x is served in a Scottish chip shop with chips, it becomes an x *supper*. What the English call "fish and chips," the Scots call a *fish supper*.

suspenders *n* garters. The things used by women to hold up their stockings. They are **not** used by men to hold up their trousers (Brits call those devices "braces") or their socks (they call those things, umm, "garters").

suss 1 *v* figure out: *I was going to try and put it back without him noticing but he sussed.* **2** *adj* dodgy; suspicious: *I really wasn't interested in buying that car... the whole deal seemed a bit suss.*

swede *n* rutabaga.

sweet 1 *n* candy: *Never take sweets from strangers, or you'll end up a dismembered corpse, rotting in a ditch like your auntie Jean.* **2** *n* dessert (particularly in restaurants).

swift half *n* a half pint of beer, had swiftly before departing. Although quite often it's not really that. You might propose having a *swift half* with some people after work, when in reality you know that it probably won't be just one *swift half*, it'll be sixteen *swift halves* like last Wednesday, when Ernie ended up

breaking his arm and you had sex with that homeless person.

swimming costume *n abbr "swimming cozzie"* bathing suit. One of those women's swimsuits that covers your midriff - not a bikini. I suppose technically there's nothing to stop men wearing them either, though that's perhaps less conventional. You can't pigeonhole me.

swizz *n* a small-scale swindle or con. If you opened your eight-pack of KitKats and there were only seven, you might mutter "that's a bloody swizz." If you discovered that your cleaning lady had been making out large cheques to herself over a ten year period, you'd be inclined to use stronger wording.

swot *n* one who studies particularly hard, usually at school. **swotting** cramming. The art of learning your complete course in one evening.

T

ta *interj* thank you. Often regarded as a little slovenly. May be derived from the Scandinavian "tak," meaning much the same thing.

table *v* put forward for discussion: *I'd like to table this for the end of the meeting.* To Americans, "table" means to put aside. Somehow these got separated, much like "momentarily."

tackle *n* male genitalia. From the fishing term "block and tackle." Use your imagination.

tailgating *n* driving too close to the car in front. In America, *tailgating* is sitting in the back of a pickup truck drinking beer and talking about NASCAR.

take-away *n* **1** take-out food: *I think we're just going to get take-away.* **2** take-out restaurant. A hot food retailer (personally I think in this instance "restaurant" is a little too strong) which only sells things that you can take home and eat or stagger down the street drunkenly stuffing in your mouth and distributing down your shirt. Blimey, that tastes good. Damnit, I've left my credit card in the pub again. Where are my keys?

taking the mickey *interj* making fun of; laughing at. Essentially a more polite version of "taking the piss."

Your grandmother would be much more likely to use this variant.

taking the piss *n* make fun of: *Andy fell down the stairs on the way into the pub last night, and everyone spent the entire night taking the piss out of him.* This is the most common term in British English to describe making fun of someone. Contrary to what one might assume, it doesn't involve a complex system of tubes or a bicycle pump.

tannoy *n* public address system. The odd name derives rather simply from the fact that a company called *Tannoy* were among the more prominent early developers of such a device.

tarmac *n* blacktop. The stuff that covers roads. Perhaps you'd like to hear some road-making history? Hmm? Or perhaps not. Perhaps you're sitting in bed naked, waiting for your husband to finish in the shower. Perhaps you're on a train in a strange foreign country, hoping that this stupid book was going to be much more of a tour guide than it turned out to be. Perhaps you're having a shit. Well, bucko, whatever you're doing you're stuck now, and so you're going to hear a little bit of road-making history. A long time ago, a Scotsman named

John Loudon Macadam invented a way of surfacing roads with gravel, this coating being known as "Macadam" - a term also used in the U.S. "What happens when the road aged?," I hear you say. Well, I'm so glad you asked. Unfortunately as the road aged the gravel tended to grind to dust and so it was coated with a layer of tar - this being "Tar-Macadam," which was concatenated to *tarmac*. Somewhere in the mists of time the Americans ended up using this only to describe airport runways, but the Brits still use it to describe the road surface.

tart *n* **1** party-girl, he says, to put it delicately. A girl easier to party on than other girls. Much the same as a "slapper," but slightly less extreme and a *little* more unisexual. *Tarts* spend hours perfecting make-up, hair and clothes before going out and waiting at the side of the dance floor to be pulled. At the end of the evening, there's a tendency for the *tarts* to slide towards slapperdom, just to make sure all that lip gloss doesn't go to waste. The word may or may not be derived from "sweetheart." **2** small cake with a filling - perhaps jam or fruit. So, when in *Alice Through the Looking Glass*, the rhyme goes "the knave of hearts, he stole the tarts," he wasn't leaping off with his arms full of easy young ladies. **3** sour (universal).

tartan *n, adj* plaid. The stripes-and-checkers pattern that Scotsmen use for their kilts but is also used for all sorts of things from throw rugs to tacky seat covers.

tater *n Northern England* potato. Not exactly sure how America ended up calling the greasy French-fry derivatives "tater tots."

tea *n* evening meal. At the risk of sounding terrible, it's just a little "working class." Maybe that doesn't sound all that terrible. There are lots of more terrible things I could say. Ask my parole officer.

tea-break *n* coffee-break. A break away from work, ostensibly to have a cup of tea, but perhaps also to have coffee or a sly fag.

tea-towel *n* dish-towel; dish-cloth. The thing you use to dry the dishes if you don't have a dishwasher. It's my belief that dishwashers are the most important invention of the twentieth century. Perhaps it'll be your belief too, now.

telly *n* TV. The term "TV" is well used and understood in the U.K., but *telly* is more common.

terrestrial television *n* regular television; cable. Any television that doesn't come from a satellite. Until recently there was no cable TV in the U.K., so any *terrestrial television* was beamed over radio waves and received by an aerial. The distinction is a bit hazy these days as the Brits are now fortunate enough to have cable TV. Nowadays, *terrestrial television* generally refers to the five channels (BBC1, BBC2, ITV, Channel Four and Channel Five) which are transmitted via radio.

tetchy *adj* touchy; irritable.

thrupney bits *n* breasts: *She was a bit dull but what a cracking pair of thrupney bits!* From Cockney rhyming slang "thrupney bits" / "tits." The *thrupney bit* was once a three-pence coin but is no longer in circulation. Although I've been doing my best to avoid putting plurals into this piece of work, I have a lot of trouble trying to think of any situation in which you would ever refer to a single *thrupney bit*. Perhaps someday the terms "thrupney bit implants" or "thrupney bit cancer" will be commonplace, but they aren't now.

tick *n* **1** check; check-mark. One of those little (usually handwritten) marks people put next to things to show that they're correct. Not the X (that's for wrong answers), the other one. **2** moment. A very short space of time, very much equivalent to the way "second" is used in conversation: *Try and hold it on for the moment, I'll be back in a tick once I've phoned an ambulance.* No doubt derived from clock noises.

tickover *n* idle (of a car engine): *It even overheats on tickover!* **ticking over** idling.

tidy *adj* a fine example of his/her gender: *Did you see the tidy new bloke working in the sweet shop?* Blokes rather like this word because it has a definite subtext suggesting dusting and hoovering.

tight *adj* **1** drunk: *My mother-in-law seemed rather nice the first time I met her, but I could swear she was tight.* **2** miserly. I'm too tired to

think of an example phrase, you'll have to make your own up.

tights *n* pantyhose. I'm getting rather out of my depth here. Opaque, very thin women's leggings and generally skin-coloured or black. "Tights" in the U.S. are generally coloured, thicker, more like leggings and rarely worn. All of this makes little difference to me because the only reason I'd ever think about buying either would be if I was considering a career in armed robbery.

till *n* cash register. The device at the checkout of a shop upon which the assistant works out how much you have to pay, and which contains the money paid by other customers. That has to be the most long-winded and hapless definition I've written lately. The word "till" is used in the U.S. but refers to the removable drawer tray in the machine, not the whole device.

tip 1 *n* place in great disarray: *Your flat is a complete tip!* Derived I think from the British term *rubbish tip*, where one goes to tip rubbish. **2** a gratuity (universal).

Tippex *n* whiteout; Liquid Paper. You know, the stuff that you use to paint over mistakes you've made on bits of paper. The stuff that smells good. Fuck, that's good. Look at the pretty colours. Who wants popcorn?

tipple *n* a demure, civilised drink. Usually of sherry, Martini or some other light spirit measure. You grandmother might acquiesce to a *tipple* before dinner. My grandmother, as it happens, acquiesced to several *tipples* before dinner, and a few after.

titchy *adj* very small; ickle. Perhaps slightly childish, but in common use in the U.K.: *Well, the food was very nice, but the helpings were titchy!*

tits up *adj* awry: *As soon as the squirrel escaped the whole thing went tits up.* Whilst the term originally referred to something which was dead (presumably derived from the orientation of said tits), it's evolved to mean anything in a poor shape.

toad in the hole *n* a delicacy consisting of sausages in Yorkshire pudding batter, in a sort of pie shape. The etymology is a tough one to guess at, as the dish itself contains no obvious holes and it's difficult, although not impossible, to confuse sausages and toads.

todger *n* penis. "Tadger," "todge" and "tadge" have been known to slip in too. As it were.

toe-rag *n* scumbag. Someone worthy of contempt - scoundrel, rotter, that sort of thing. A rather antiquated word, it may come from a time where dockers used to stuff rags into their boots in order to keep out wheat seeds, which hurt a lot if you get one in your shoe. I've never put any wheat in my shoes to test the theory. Just as soon as this makes me rich, I'll start making it better-informed. Another possible etymology is that it was originally "tow rag," which was a piece of cloth used for mopping up oil.

toff *n* member of the upper classes - someone born with a silver spoon

in their mouth, you might say. A rather esoteric working-class term.

tomato sauce *n* tomato ketchup. In the U.K. these two terms are interchangeable although "tomato ketchup" is in more common use, as *tomato sauce* could equally easily refer to the pasta-type sauce in a jar or can.

toodle-pip *interj* goodbye; cheerio. Rather old-fashioned. Also **toodle-oo**. This may be derived from English soldiers attempting to pronounce "a tout à l'heure" ("see you later") in French during the First World War. Or perhaps *toodle-pip* is some sort of derivation of that involving the French word "pipe," which is slang for a blow-job. Whilst this fact is true, the derivation idea is something I've just made up off the top of my head right now.

torch 1 *n* flashlight. The word originally referred to real burning torches and so ... **2** *v* ...has also developed into a verb meaning "to set fire to": *Diego's mate fucked us over with the DVD deal so we torched the place.*

tosh *adj* rubbish; nonsense: *Katie's new boyfriend was going on about how he works in high finance somewhere - personally, I think it's all a load of tosh.*

toss *v* masturbate. To call someone a *tosser* is to suggest that they are an accomplished onanist. The word was originally in use as *tosser* or "toss-pot" to describe a drunk (tossing one-too-many drinks back) but, as with most things, has

become more gloriously sordid.
give a toss give a shit.

totty *n* attractive members of the opposite sex: *Well, I'm definitely going there again. Wall-to-wall totty.* Not said by me, of course.

trailer tent *n* pop-up camper. A sort of folding-up caravan. It starts off as an average-sized trailer and then unfolds into a sort of crappy shed when you reach a campsite.

trainers *n* sneakers; running shoes.

train-spotter 1 *n* a person whose hobby is to, well, spot trains. They stand in railway stations or on bridges and note down the types and serial numbers of any trains that go past. I was fortunate enough to be in Reading Station one afternoon while a train-spotting convention was in town; the place was a sea of bright yellow reflective jackets and they had video cameras set up on each platform. Perhaps it's a social thing. Anyway, the term was made a household one by Irvine Welsh's excellent book, *Trainspotting*, which is not about spotting trains. **2** *n* nerd. Stemming directly from the prior definition, this word has come to mean anyone who is a little too engrossed in one particular none-too-interesting subject, and probably a virgin.

tram *n* streetcar; trolley. A device very much like a train except it generally runs on tracks built on top of normal roads and is often powered electrically by high-strung cables (I mean ones on poles, not ones of an excitable disposition). Trams are making something of a

comeback in Europe generally, with new systems springing up in the U.K.

tramp *n* bum; homeless person. Brits don't use the term "bum" in this context.

treacle *n* molasses.

trilby *n* a mens' felt-type hat (generally brown). I don't know much about hats, so can't enlighten you much more. Really, I wish I could. It's just not within my power.

trolley *n* shopping cart. The device in which you put your shopping while going around the supermarket. What Americans call "trolleys," the Brits call "trams."

trolley dolly *n* air stewardess. I'm sure you'll work it out.

trolleyed *adj* extremely drunk. Perhaps the term came from something to do with ending up in hospital. No idea.

trollop *n* woman of loose morals. This is a somewhat antiquated equivalent of "tart," and was sixteenth-century slang for a prostitute.

trousers *n* pants. In the U.K., "pants" are underpants, and so being "caught with your pants down" has even more graphic connotations.

truncheon *n* The baton used by policemen to quieten down rowdy charges. The Brits still have sticks, whilst many American police forces have replaced them with unusually heavy flashlights.

Tube *n* the London Underground railway. Londoners are clearly not as inspired as Glaswegians, who call theirs the "Clockwork

Orange." In the U.S., these sorts of rail systems are known as "subways" which, no doubt in order to cause confusion, is what the Brits call the walkways which go underneath roads, where tramps live and drunk people urinate.

tuck shop *n* candy store. Derived from the word "shop," which means "store." And also the word "tuck."

twat 1 *n* female genitalia. Not to be used in overly-polite company. The word, I mean. **2** *v* thump; hit: *I don't remember anything after the boom swung around and I got twatted.* **3** *n* idiot. Generally directed at blokes. A suitably confusing example would read "some twat in the pub accused me of having been near his bird's twat, so I twatted him." On the female genitalia front, so to speak, the poet Robert Browning once read a rather vulgar protestant polemic which referred to an "old nun's twat," and subsequently mentioned a nun's "cowl and twat" in one of his poems, under the mistaken impression that it was a part of her clothing.

twee *adj* kitsch. Old ladies' front rooms, tartan cloth jackets and pleasant little sleepy retirement towns are *twee*. Marilyn Manson, drive-by-shootings and herpes are not.

twig *v* catch on; realise that something is up: *Bob just poured the contents of the ashtray into Fred's pint but he's so pissed I doubt he'll twig.* It may come from

the Gaelic word "tig," meaning "understand."

twit *n* twerp; nitwit. Made famous by Roald Dahl's book *The Twits*, about a rather obnoxious couple of them.

two up, two down *n* a house with two rooms upstairs and two downstairs. A one-up, one-down is an even smaller house.

twonk *n* idiot. There seem to be more ways of politely describing your friends as mentally deficient in British English than anything else.

tyke *n* rascal; tearaway. Normally used to describe children who are doing something a bit mischievous but not particularly awful. You'd be much more likely to hear "Quit spraying me with the hose, you wee tyke!" than you would "Run, the little tyke's got a bomb!"

tyre *n* tire. The black rubber things around the wheels of your car. The British spelling in this particular instance is, well, curious.

U

underground *n* subway (specifically underground railway): *There's an underground station two minutes from my house.*

underlay *n* carpet pad. As far as Americans are concerned, the "underlay" is the wood that lies underneath the carpet pad.

university *n* college. As well as having the "University of St. Andrews" in the same way that Americans would have the "University of Oklahoma," Brits use *university* as a general term to describe those sorts of institutions: *I'm still at university at the moment.* Brits do not use the word "college" in that context.

uphill gardener *n* homosexual. Perhaps best left at that.

up the duff *n* pregnant: *Did you hear Judith's up the duff again?*

V

verge *n* shoulder. The edge of the road, populated by hitch-hikers, frogs and children urinating. That's "frogs" and "children urinating," not "(frogs and children) urinating." Glad I could clear that up. Let me know if you have any other questions.

vest *n* undershirt. The item of clothing worn under your shirt. What Americans call a "vest," Brits call a "waistcoat."

video 1 *n* VCR: *I left it in the living room sitting on top of the video.* And yes, they do call the tapes "videos" too. These days the general concept of a video tape is fading into the distant past as DVD takes over. Perhaps eventually I'll remove this. **2** *v* record onto videotape: *Mary and I spent the weekend videoing the neighbours copulating.*

W

waffle *n, v* banal or rambling conversation. You might describe your CEO's yearly speech to the employees as nothing more than *waffle*, and likewise you could accuse him of *waffling*. Brits do describe those cross-hatched baked batter things as "waffles," but they don't really eat them all that much.

waistcoat *n* vest. An odd sort of article of clothing worn over your shirt but under your jacket, often with a bow-tie. In the U.K., "vest" means something else, as usual.

wally *n* dimwit; dunce. In a friendly sort of a way. You'd never leap out of your car after someone's smashed into the back of it and shout "you complete fucking wally!"

wank *v* masturbate. **wanker** *n* one who masturbates. Quite a rude word in the U.K. - perhaps one notch worse than "fuckwit" on the international offensiveness scale I've just invented. Interesting, therefore, that Adam Clayton of U2 managed to get away with using it in a *Simpsons* episode and that Phil Collins managed to use it in his 1984 *Miami Vice* cameo.

washing up *n* washing the dishes: *Let me help with the washing up!* **washing up liquid** dish soap.

waster *n* someone who just sits around watching television and spending their income support on dope. Presumably derived in some way from "time-waster."

wazzack *n* idiot. When I originally put this on my website I spelled it "wazzak." I received emails variously informing me that it was spelled "wazzock" or "wuzzock." I then received one from a chap who claimed to have invented the word in South Somerset when he was seven and that "wazzack" was in fact the correct spelling. And the one I got from a chap in Nottinghamshire claiming that he invented it and it was spelled "wassak." Why must society be like this? Why must we all lay claim to something? I put the two people in touch via email and they have subsequently fallen in love.

W.C. *n* toilet. A currently-used acronym which stands for the not-so-currently used term "water closet." This term stems from a time early in toilet development when they were nothing more than a carefully waterproofed cupboard filled halfway up with seawater. Not to be confused with a "W.P.C." (Woman Police Constable).

wean *n Scottish* child. Derived from the colloquial Scots "wee 'un" (little one).

wee 1 *adj Scottish* small: *That's an awfully wee car - are you sure you'll all fit in it?* In a loose sense it could also be interpreted as meaning "cute" in the "cute and cuddly" sense. You could tell someone they had a "nice wee dog," but might meet with more curious glances if you used it in a more serious scenario: *"Well, Mrs. Brown, I'm sad to tell you that you have a wee tumour on your cerebral cortex."* **2** *v* urinate: *Back in a minute, I'm going to have a wee.*

wellies *n* Wellington boots. Look it up. It can't be far.

Wellingtons *n* rubber boots; galoshes. A contraction of the term "Wellington boots," which was the inventive name given to boots made popular by the Duke of Wellington. The further abbreviation "wellies" is also in common use.

welly *n Scottish* (when talking about automobiles) stick; punch: *If you give it some welly you'll hit fifty through the corners!* This may or may not be related to the "wellington boot" definition.

what's up? *interj* what's wrong? While this means something akin to "hello" in the U.S., Brits use it to mean "what is wrong with you?"

whinge *v* whine: *Ah, quit whinging, for heaven's sake!* **whinger** someone particularly partial to whinging.

whip round *n* passing the hat. A collection of money - usually a somewhat impromptu and informal one. You might have a *whip round* for Big Mike's bus-fare home but you probably wouldn't have one for his triple heart bypass. Unless you were using it as an attempt to bring a spot of humour to an otherwise morbid situation in the sort of way my wife doesn't like me trying to do.

wholemeal flour *n* whole-wheat/whole-grain flour. I've no idea about food; I hope it's not apparent. I just type what people tell me like a big unpaid secretary.

wicked *adj* cool; awesome: *Jim's got a wicked new car stereo.* A little bit eighties. Okay, a lot eighties.

willie *n* penis. The film *Free Willie* attracted large optimistic female audiences when it was released in the U.K. That could either mean audiences of large optimistic females, or large audiences of optimistic females. Either way it's a lie. Of perhaps more amusement to Brits was the 1985 American film *Goonies*, which featured a group of children who found a secret pirate-ship commanded by a fearsome pirate named One-Eyed-Willie. Or how about the Alaskan car-wash company, *Wet Willies*, who offer two levels of service named *Little Willie* and *Big Willie*? Seems something of a no-brainer.

windscreen 1 *n* windshield (of a car). **2** *n* one of those things that you put up on a beach that stops the sand from blowing in and stops those inside from noticing that the tide is coming in.

wing *n* fender. The metal part of a car that covers the front wheel and joins onto the bonnet. Perhaps it derives from the time when cars were made which could fly.

wizard *adj* cool; awesome: *Wow! That's wizard!* A bit eighties. I have to emphasise here that just because words are in the dictionary doesn't mean to say I use them on a regular basis. As far as I'm concerned it has a similar aura to "Bitchin'!"

wobbler *n* fit of anger. **throwing a -** same sort of thing.

wobbly *n* Used in the same way as "wobbler."

wonky *adj* not quite right. You might say "My plans for the evening went a bit wonky"; you would not say "I'm sorry to tell you, Mr. Jones, but your wife's cardiac operation has gone a bit wonky." The American English word "wonk" (an expert in some particular subject) is not used in the U.K.

woofter *n* homosexual. Yet another term for a homosexual, in case the Brits needed some more.

woolly *adj* ill-defined; vague: *We gave up halfway through his presentation... it all seemed a bit woolly.*

wotcher *interj* howdy; hey there. A form of greeting, rather more familiar to Victorian schoolboys than anyone more contemporary. Harks back to a time when "cock" meant something like "mate," but nowadays marching into a bar and greeting someone with "wotcher, cock!" is unlikely to make you more popular.

Y

Yank *n, adj* American. To a Brit, a *Yank* is anyone of American descent. It's not altogether complimentary and conjures up an image of Stetsons, oil wells, Cadillacs and overweight children. The word comes from "Yankee" - after receiving and trying to synopsize nearly a million different explanations for where *that* word came from, I realised that I was drifting wildly off topic and so I've scrubbed them all. Go and look it up elsewhere. **yank tank** American car. A description one might regard as unfair to the humble tank.

Yardies *n* a London criminal gang. The name originated (with the gang) in Jamaica, where drug barons lived in downtown Kingston in homes build inside high-walled yards.

Y-fronts *n* briefs. The more form-fitting old-fashioned equivalent of boxer shorts. The name derives from the upside-down 'Y' shape on the front, through the convergence of which you extract your old man in order to pee.

yobbo *n* hooligan; rabble-rouser. Usually seen in the context of upper-middle-class people referring to the working-classes: *Well, yes, Mildred - my Jeremy used to be such a sensible boy but now he's got mixed up with this awful crowd of yobbos!* The derivation of the word is apparently modified back-slang - the moniker "boyo" became "yobbo." Amusingly, in New York City slang, "yobbos" are breasts. Not in the U.K.

yonks *n* a long time; ages. Not a specific length of time at all; it could be minutes or decades: *Where have you been? I've been waiting here for yonks!* or: *Met a friend from school the other day that I haven't seen for yonks.*

Z (Zed)

zebra crossing *n* the black-and-white striped pathways drawn across roads where pedestrians have right of way and motorists have to stop if anyone is waiting by them. The phrase has been slightly usurped by the less exciting term "pedestrian crossing." While this very concept of "it's alright, on you go, the cars all have to stop" is dangerous enough, a great deal of them are positioned straight after roundabouts where motorists are least likely to be ready for them. I swear these things are part of some sort of population control policy. To make them marginally easier to see, some of them are marked with Belisha Beacons.

zed *n* Z. The letter that the Americans pronounce "zee," the Brits pronounce "zed." Products with the super-snappy prefix "EZ" added to their names don't tend do quite so well in the U.K. And yes, this does mean that British schoolchildren never hear the "alphabet song" that ends "now I know my A-B-C / next time won't you sing with me?" as it relies somewhat on the G / P / V / Z rhyme. Perhaps G, P and V could be renamed "ged," "ped" and "ved" in order to adopt it. I might write to the education minister saying as much.

Zimmer *n* **also "Zimmer frame"** walker. One of those four-legged frame devices that the elderly use in order to help them get around the place. Zimmer is the brand name of a manufacturer of these things.

CONTRIBUTORS

The dictionary portion of this fine piece of work is an internet-based project, available for the rest of time at http://english2american.com. Well, maybe not for the rest of time. In fact, I'd warrant that what you're reading now will last longer than the one that's on the internet. I can't see the wife sitting paying my ISP subscription when I'm six feet under. Anyway, the fact that it is an Internet Thing means that most of the ideas were not mine, but instead stolen from innocent members of the public. As I worked on it (let's be honest, not very hard), a steady stream of emails arrived from angry readers complaining that I'd got something wrong or omitted something.

As time went on, the backlog of ideas grew larger and larger with no obvious end in sight, like some sort of awful killing spree. Eventually I hit upon the idea of forcing people to buy me beer if they wanted me to read their emails. Remarkably, several people succumbed and I posted pictures of myself drinking their beers on the website. It seems only fair to reproduce them here.

I can tell you're wondering about the ordering. The people who paid the most for their beers are at the top. Yes, I realise this doesn't favour people who bought more than one beer but it turned out that was going to play havoc with my database and it's 3am and I'm tired and I'm trying to get this thing to the printers and goddamnit, do you have nothing better to do with your life? Sit back and take a look at yourself. Jesus.

The Septic's Companion

The Septic's Companion

Sam Shublom

Sarabeth Thomas

Sarah Casey

Sarah Ellerton

Sarah MacKenzie

Sten Severson

Suzanne Hardy

Tom Evans

Tracy Brooks

David Barnett

Jeremy Stamp

Lawrence Johnson

Nicholas McWilliam

Lexi H.

Ellen Gragg

Cooperative Maine Craftsmen

Paul Pagett

Wendy Woolpert

Mike Francesconi

Also, sans beer: Aaron C. Meyer, Aaron Harder, Adam Pearce, Adam Seale, Adrianne Johnson, Aida, Ailsa Parr, Aimé F. Watts Jr, AJ, Al, Alan, Alan Benedict, Alan Eldred, Alan Harrison, Alan Holm, Alanna J Edwards, Alastair Hammond, Alberto J. Miyara, Alec Smith, Aleks, Alex, Alex Protopopescu, Alexander Deubelbeiss, Alexandra Patten, Ali Hill, Alicia Garbe, Alick Reid, Alistair Philpott, ALM135, Alyssa, Alyssa Elliott, Amanda E. Ribera, Amber, Amber Wood, Amy Jordan, Amy Smith, Amy Thompson, Andrea, Andrea Caldecourt, Andrea Warren, Andrew Cline, Andrew Crane, Andrew Crofts, Andrew Crompton, Andrew Holgate, Andrew Johnson, Andrew Lambert, Andrew McConkey, Andrew Meador, Andrew Perrett, Andrew Saddington, Andrew Sharkey, Andy Behrens, Andy Head, Andy Jenkinson, Andy Jerison, Andy Monks, Andy Stocks, Andy Wain, Andyaz, AndyT13, Angela, Angela (the Book Dragon), Angela Johnson, Ann, Ann Fink, Anna J-L, Anna M. Josenhans, Anne Krone, Anne Runkle, Anno v. Heimburg, Anthony Poole, Appleseed, April, Arie van der Velden, Arijan, Arne Heizmann, Arturo Rios Jr, Ashley, Ashley Black, Astral, Audrey, B.J. Herbison, Bake01, Barbara Hill, Barry, Bayard, Bee Yinn Low, Beldon Dominello, Belinda Webb, ben, Ben Brosgol, Ben Butzer, Bernardette Heaps, Beth Chirilov, Beth Gerty, Betty Moreno, Bil Voyce, Bill Allen, Bill Berg, Bill Bruce, Bill Buffam, Bill Drissel, Bill Hughes, Bill Miramontes, Bill Rentiers, Bill Robinson, Bill Scott, Bill Varnedoe, Blaine Emmett, Blair Peery, Bloodbat, Bob, Bob Burbeck, Bob Caddick, Bob McCalden, Bob Monfort, Boidster, Boris Jabes, Bort, Brad Schewe, Brandon Jenkins, Brandy, Bree Turner, Brendan Hogg, Brendon, Brent Shook, Brent W. Adams, Brett Reid Parker, Brian A. Rogers, Brian Abernathy, Brian C. DeRocher, Brian Canada, Brian Carter, Brian Foley, Brian Gainor, Brian Haunton, Brian Holcomb, Brian Jacobs, Brian Lang, Brian Mastenbrook, Brian Otridge, Brian Sturrock, Brian Thompson, Britany Escalera, Brooke Jones, Bruce Darton, Bruce Hazen, Bryan Dorland, Bryony, Bun Burns, Burt, Burton F. Urquhart, Carl Moss, Carl Tostevin, Carmen Sternwood, Carol Zupfer, Carolyn Craig, Carolyn Deans, Carrie Hall, Cat Simmons, Catherine Molanphy, Catherine Waechter, Cathleen Graham, Cathy, Cathyn R. Lesanges, Caz Lee, cerebus12, Cesca, Charles Armstrong, Charles H. Budd, Charles Mercadal, Charles Neveu, Charlie Adlum, Charmaine Haith, Chas, Cheryl Pierce, ChicletteX, Chris, Chris Akin, Chris Cartwright, Chris Chambers, Chris Cooper, Chris Eccleston, Chris Hatton, Chris Kindschi, Chris Linfoot, Chris Maynard, Chris Means, Chris Nichols, Chris Qugley, Chris Stanley, Chris Vandemore, Christian Carbines, Christine, Christine Davis, Christine Forber, Christine Forte, Christopher R. Maden, Christopher Smith, Christopher Wood, Chuck Coopman, Chuck Yurkonis, Cindy, Clara , Clare Ring, Clark, Coleman W. Sleeper, Colin Davies, Colin Leigh, Colin McCallum, Colin McGeechan, Colin McQueen, Connie Lehigh Acres, Connor Neely, Cori Bird, Cornelius Canton, Cort Tompkins, Courtlandt Monte Zepeda, Craig Cottingham, Crystal, Cyndi, Cynthia Balfour-Traill, Cynthia Rose Kahn, D. Goldrich, D. Nathan Rice, D. Roberts, D.B. James, Dafydd Williams, Damien Oxley, Dan Mick, Dan Ozenberger, Dan Q, Dan Walker, Daniel Cochran, Daniel Hawthorn, Daniel Roan, Daniel Vazquez, Danielle, Dara, Darin Sides, Darrell Morrow, Darren Logan, Darren Moore, Dave, Dave Carter, Dave Collins, Dave Haworth, Dave Johnson, Dave Purdy, Dave Scott, Dave Williams, David, David Boone, David Brodbeck, David Flanagan, David Ford, David Gainer, David Gallie, David Gilby, David Harper, David Hecht, David Henry, David Jeffrey, David Kilkelly, David Loewe, David Martinez, David Odell, David Smedley, David Staudacher, David Strother, David Zviel, Dawn Reynolds, Debbe Dobson, Debbie Lange, DeeDee, Denice Donnelly, Dennis Esters, Dennis Forbes, Derek Mulcahy, Diane Fisher, Diane Russell, Digger, Dik Langan, Dinah, Dobbin, Don Schwarz, Don Tanner, Don Upton, Donald J. Manthei, Dormouse, Doug Harper, Douglas Yates, Duncan Mallet, Dusty, E. J. Hogan, Earl Dunbar, Ed Grigoleit, Ed Infurna, Ed Ingram, Ed Roberts, Ed Uber, Eddie Philpott-Kent, Edel, Edmund Broadley, Edward Lockhart, Edward Tombari, El Bandito, Elaine, Eleanor Nabney, Elizabeth Andrews, Elizabeth Doherty, Ellen, Ellen Lind, Emily, Emily Patrick, Eric Breck, Eric J Iannelli, Eric Katz,M.D., Eric Kieboom, Erica Jackson, Erik, Erika, Erika Hitsman, Erin Kellett, Ernest Bramah, Ernest Perez, Ernie Schell, Esther Nairn, Eye, Fionnuala Doyle, Fisher, Frances & David Stocks, Frances Lynn, Francesco Vitelli, Francisco De Freitas, Frank, Frank Calise, Frank Lynch, Fraser Moore, Fred Spaulding, Fritz Barnes, Ganymede, Gareth, Gareth J Barnard, Gary Glynn-Springer, Gary North, Gary Whitehead, Gary Wyatt, Gavin Whitlock, Gay Cannon, gbh65, Gel, Geoff, Geoff Berrow, Geoff Cook, Geoff Hill, George Bolgar, George Finlay, George Kirchwey, George Strasser, Gerry Thomson, Gillian Taylor, Gina Marquez, Glenna, Gnu, Golux, Gordon Cruickshank, Gordon O'Connor, Graham Hays, Graham Lattin, Graham Thomas, Grant O. J., Greg Chandler, Greg Delott, Greg Goss, Greg Kaighin, Greg Larson, Gregg Senne, Gretchen Strauch, Groda, Gryffin, Guy Bowerman, Guy Seven, Gwenda Stewart, Hamish Brown, Hannah Dentinger, Harold Kruitbosch, Harry Blanchard, Harry Rueckel, Hazel Muir, Heather Glude, Helen Bryant, Helen Griffin, Helena, Henrik Jonsson, Henry Moffitt, Henry Mullan, Henry O'D Thompson, Henry P. Hunsperger, Highlander, Hisashi T Fujinaka, Hodo, Holly Button, Hooman Ganjavi, Howard Crosslen, Hrvoje Niksic, Hugo Mills, Iain, Iain Farrell, Iain Harrison, Iain Tatch, Ian Davidson, Ian Forknall, Ian Johnson, Ian Nisbet, Ian Oglesby, Ian Peacock, Ian Strange, Ian Tullock, India, Inken Purves, Iqbal, Isabella Ranbom, Jaap Weel, Jacqueline Glisson, Jacquelyne Lord, Jadawin, Jade Brown, Jade Hammons, Jake Aard, Jakob Bronebakk, James, James Cloninger, James Hardy, James M. De Arras, James Nelson-Parker, James O'Connell, James Rivera, James Robinson, James S. George, Jami JoAnne Russell, Jamie, Jamie Logan, Jana, Jane Funka, Jane Lavendar, Jane Wolfarth, Janet Bass, Janet Clancy, Janet Hall, Janice Rosenberg, Janine Blackwolf, Jarrod, Jason Blatt, Jason Collings, Jason Kirkfield, Jason Marshall, Jason Weill, Jay Galvin, Jay L. Jones, Jay Martin, Jay Shaffer, Jaybee, Jean Ryba, Jeanette Biermann, Jeb Boyd, Jef Raber, Jeff, Jeff Bishop, Jeff Schulze, Jeff Smith, Jeff Spindler, Jeff Thomas, Jen, Jeneen Hercho, Jennifer, Jennifer Antrim, Jennifer Personius, Jennifer Ranwez, Jennifer Sandlin, Jennifer Simonds, Jennifer Wiginton, Jenny Dean, Jens Johansen, Jeremy Eble, Jeremy Pankratz, Jernau Gurgeh, Jerry Baker, Jerry Hutton, Jessica, Jill Boyce, Jill Bradford, Jim, Jim Calvert, Jim Fuckwit, Jim Michnowicz, Jim Pollock, Jim Yonemura, JJ, Joanne Morris, Jodi Fisher, Joe, Joe Chirilov (beer photographer), Joe Griffey, Joe Leitch, Joe Sabo, Johan, John Bowen, John Burgess, John Coathupe, John D. French, John Draper, John Green, John Gwatkin-Williams, John H, John Harrington, John Hasler, John Ings, John Jelinski, John Kelly, John L. Birch, John Manning, John Matthews, John McCarron, John McMullen, John Nisbet, John Payne, John Qualmann, John Semple, John Slater, John Smart, John Trickey, John Twernbold, John Woods, JohnnyTreachery, John-Paul, Jon, Jon Bartlett, Jon Gross, Jon J., Jon Marx, Jonah, Jonathan R. Mills, Jonathon Furse, Jory, Joseph Crone, Joseph Wright, Josh Audette, Joshua Miller, Joy Byford, J'Raxis, Judy, Judy Battista, Julia Milton, Julia Morgan, Julia Novak, Julian Nicholls, Julian Sheffield, Juliane, Julie, Júlio Reis, Justin Nichols, Justin Waugh, Jyri Erik Kork, Karen Mora, Karl Dane, Karl Doll, Karl Liander, Karlita7, Karolyne "DSM" Marcil, Kate Fleischer, Kate Macfadyen, Kate Steiner, Kate Tuckwell, Katerina Grelle, Kath, Katherine Crosswhite, Katherine Levin, Kathy Guernsey, Kathy H., Kathy Kelly, Kathy Pappas, Kathy S., Katie Clayton, Katie Hawthorne, Katie Ringland, Kay Murgatroyd, Keith Crossley, Keith Macdonald, Kelly, Kelly Billingsley, Kelly Porpiglia, Kelsey Wiff, Ken Jones, Ken Marks, Kenny Anderson, Kent K. Steinbrenner, Kent Spackman, Kerri, Kerry Kartchner, Kevin Davis (AWESOME), Kevin Jundt, Kevin Purcell, Kevin Quinn, Kevin Salger, Kiera McNichols, Kieran Ball, Kiki, Kiki Rae, Kim Brown, Kim Major, Kimberly, Koko, Kristen, Kristian Harms, Kristina Plath, Krun, Krystal, Kurt Ramsauer, Kyle Goetz, L Murray, L. Hutcheson, Lance Henderson, Larry Schiereck, Laura Conover, Laura DeVere, Lauren Morfoot, Laurie McFarland, Lee, Lee Tostevin, Len, Leonard Priestley, Leslie, Leslie E. Hubanks, Lexie, Liesl Gray, Lili, Linda, Linda Death, Linda Ericson, Linda F Lindenfelser, Linda Griffith, Lisa Patterson, Liz Moog, Liz Wong, Llij, Loanne Rodney, Lori Kreckow, Lorri Cusson, Louisa, Louise Bach, Louise Peterkin, Loyd J. Brown, Lucy Phillips, Luke Burnham, Lynn Walters, Madeleine Price, Maggie Jones, Maitreya Maziarz, Mandy, Manuel Canut, Mara, Marc Kinzelman, Marcelo Siqueira Gonçalves, Margaret Hollendoner, Margaret Lattany, Margie, Marguerite Eras, Mari, Maria Day, Maria Grazia Navacchia, Marianne Fox, Marie Jones, Marjorie Douty, Marjorie Parent-Greenman, Mark, Mark Abbott, Mark Amrhein, Mark Coletti, Mark Eckenwiler, Mark Guenther, Mark Moss, Mark Oglesby, Mark O'Hare, Mark Parris, Mark Patterson, Mark Rudden, Mark Shah, Mark Southwell, Martin DeMello, Martin Gutkowski, Martin Nutt, Martin Watts, Mary Goodearl, Mary Powers, Mary W., Matt Boothman, Matt Dowden, Matt Karlsson, Matt Sullivan, Matt Sweger, Matthew Bireta, Matthew Denniston, Matthew M, Matthew Trentini, Maureen Boyd, Mavis Hoffman, Max Waterman, Max Wurr, Maximus Roberts, Mayke, Me me, Meg, Megan Burgess, Mel, Melissa Allen, Melissa Schall Willmore, Meredith Wilson, Meredydd Luff, Mic Marcroft, Micah Nutt, Michael, Michael Angelo Ravera, Michael Barry, Michael Brennan, Michael Deatherage, Michael Galletly, Michael Gelose, Michael Kneis, Michael Licata, Michael McDavid, Michael McGovern, Michael Mosbey, Michael Pepper, Michael Stewart, Michael Wright, Michele Goldstein, Michele Mantynen, Michelle, Mickey Blake, Mickey McDonough, Midnightmouse624, Mike, Mike Allaway, Mike and Colleen Spence, Mike Anderson, Mike Bailey, Mike Bond, Mike Bristow, Mike deFreitas, Mike Diamond, Mike Down, Mike Green, Mike Hawkes, Mike J, Mike Kordosky, Mike Maher, Mike Perrin, Mike Schmidt, Mike Steele, Mike Z, Mila, Milly Hopkins, Mippy, Miracle Ace, Miranda Oakley, Miriam Himmelfarb, Miriam Mohammed, Misshisss, Monty Christiansen, Mordechai Brown, Mutt Baskerville, Myronda, N. J. O'Neill, Nancy Kane, Nancy Miller, Nancy Tajjioui, Nathan Azinger, Nathan Sharfi, Neil Baus, Neil Jones, Neil Kent, Neil Kirsopp, Neil Morris, Neil Reddy, Nev Phillips, Nic Percival, Nicemandan, Nicholas Byram, Nick Cooke, Nick Doak, Nick Simons, Nick Smith, Nicola Hodgson, Nicola Murphy, Nicole Albert, Nicole M. Bigas, Nigel A.Gunn, Nigel Asquith, Nigel S., Nikki, Nimrod Fartelchease, Nina, ninjaTED, Noel Mooney, Nora Gruenberg, Oliver Pattenden, Owen, Palacio, Pamela L. Story, Pamela Speak, Pat Bitton, Pat Davies, Pat McAloon, Pat O'Donnell, Patch, Patricia Beck, Patrick Carroll, Patrick Croson, Patrick Devitt, Patrick Rock, Patrick Rowley, Pattie Lee, Paul, Paul Cave, Paul Ciszek, Paul Durrant, Paul E. Denel, Paul Greenwood, Paul Gush, Paul Hoernes, Paul Johns, Paul Lomax, Paul Makin, Paul Marcroft, Paul Nation, Paul Sawers, Paul Sawyer, Paul Shepherd, Paula Cohen, Penni, Pete Green, Pete Jones, Peter Bailey, Peter Belew, Peter Bradley, Peter Chung, Peter Donaldson, Peter Gravelle, Peter Hazen, Peter Hyde,

The Septic's Companion

Peter Lines, Peter McCrorie, Phil Braham, Phil Brennan, Phil Hardy, Phil Swan, Phil Underwood, Phineas Campbell, Prateep Bandharangshi, Rae, Raelinn, Rainbo, Randy, Rashell Beya, Raven Reeves, Ray, Ray Seamans, Rebecca, Rebecca Lamey, Redvers Davies, Reg Gothard, Renee Hayes, Rhoda Rosenthal, Rhys, Richard Anstess, Richard Aston, Richard Floyd, Richard Howell, Richard Saady, Rick Harley, Rick Seddon, Rob Abram, Rob Branston, Rob Gordon, Rob Gronotte, Rob King, Rob Naylor, Rob Pearce, Rob Williams, Rob Wingfield, Robert Beckett, Robert Evans, Robert How, Robert James, Robert Pitt, Robert Poirier, Robert Setnicka, Robert Stephenson, Robert Thomson, Robin, Robin Coolbeth, Robin Fish, Robin McCall, Robin Valk, Rochelle, Roger Ashford, Roger Bryant, Roger Fratti, Roland Tomlinson, Ron Russell, Ronkenator, Ros, Rosalind Mehra, Roschelle, Roslyn Mclean, Ru Ru, RumpusBloke, Russell Bailinson, Ryan McMinn, Sam Giffin, Sam Johnson, Sam Seifers, Sandra Giarde, Sandra McHugh, Sandro, Sandy, Sandy Guthrie, Sandy McDaniel, Santiago Fittipaldi, Sara Howland, Sarah, Sarah Brown, Sarah Charman, Sarah Hayman, Sarah Knight-Hassell, Sarah Panzer, Sarah Wren, Scot Bogart, Scott Allen Miller, Scott Brookes, Scott Ely, Scott Shipley, Scott Stephens, Scott Stevenson, Scott Troiano, Scott W. Langill, Sean, Sean Tibbitts, Selkie, Shamsul Shaikh, Shannon, Sharon, Sharon Damoff, Sharon Jones, Sharon Marcussen, Sheila, Sheila B. Auster, Shelley, Sheridan Kulwicki, Shirleyann Soltys, Si Cochrane, Simon, Simon Ahern, Simon D'Cruz, Simon Howard, Simon Levene, Simon Murph, Sir Dom Tom, Skip Flem, Skip Orr, Smahon, Sng Swee Huat, Sparky Smith, Spicy Pizza, Stacey Fullwiler, Stacey Lind, Stan Brown, Stefan Malmesjö, Stephen Baxter-Smith, Stephen Edwards, Stephen Gallagher, Stephen Gibson, Stephen James, Stephen Jeffcoat, Stephen Montgomery-Smith, Stephen Tonkin, Steve C, Steve Greenberg, Steve Harrynuk, Steve Herrick, Steve James, Steve Mackay, Steve Painter, Steve Robb, Steve Rose, Steve Sosensky, Steven, Steven C. Den Beste, Steven Rogers, Stewart Rose, Stewart Stevens, Stfan Muramaa, Stina Babbitt, Stuart, Stuart Anderson, Stuart Donaldson, Stuart Johnson, Stuart Light, Stuart McConnachie, Stuart Wardell, Summer, Sumo, Susan Chang, Susan Hollis Merritt, Susan Paterson, Susan Raby, Suzanne Adams, Suzanne S. Barnhill, Suzanne Shukri, Suzi Fraser Dominy, T. Ellis, T. Gilles, Tania Hewes, Tara O'Byrne, Teresa Hickam, Terrence Hancock, Terry, Theodore Galanis, Thibaut Vial, Thomas Luby, Thomas Paul, Thomas Ronayne, Tim, Tim Adams, Tim Allison, Tim Dellert, Tim Gonyou, Tim Harcourt, Tim Nelson, Timon, Timothy Leuers, Tina Dodgen, Toby Bunyan, Todd Drain, Tom, Tom Miraldi, Tom Raptis, Tonie, Tony D'Agostino, Tony Lavender, Tony Herring, Trevor Henry, Tripper, Troy, Twitch, Tycho Manson, Ulysses Hillard, Valerie, Vanessa McKenzie, Vince Wald, Vincent Kane, Vinny, W. Jansen, Walt Staves, Warren Brunson, Wayne Jenness, Wayne Moore, Wendi, Will Carpenter, William Lucking, William Yeates, Willicus Maximus, Witho, Wubba Wubba, Zed and Zoeanne.

Printed in the United States
131453LV00001B/50/P

9 780981 579009